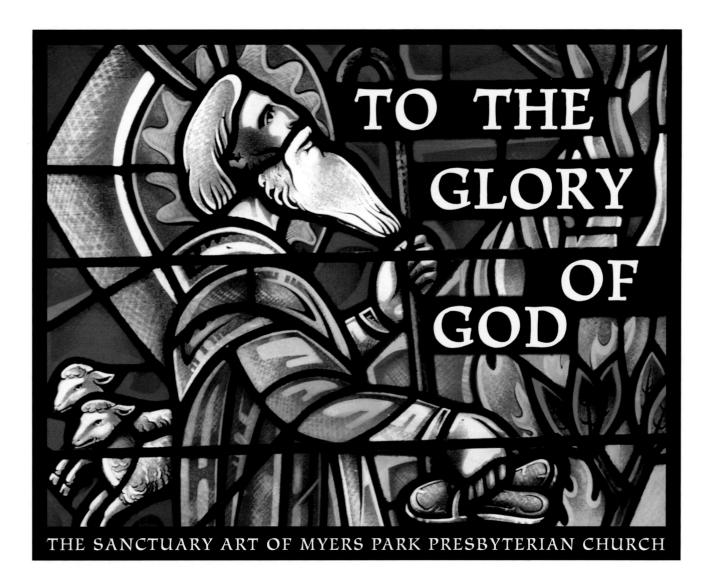

TO THE
GLORY
OF
GOD

THE SANCTUARY ART OF MYERS PARK PRESBYTERIAN CHURCH

To The Glory of God
The Sanctuary Art of Myers Park Presbyterian Church

Copyright © 2003

Published by Myers Park Presbyterian Church
Charlotte, North Carolina

Printed by Jostens
Charlotte, North Carolina

Additional credits listed on page 112 are considered a continuation of this copyright page.

First edition

Photography by Gordon Schenck

Reorder Information:
Myers Park Presbyterian Church
2501 Oxford Place
Charlotte, North Carolina 28207

Front Cover: Depicts Moses standing before the burning bush. The Moses window, detailed beginning on page 17, can be found in the sanctuary of Myers Park Presbyterian Church in the third window on the lectern side.

Back Cover: Portrays the baby Jesus of Joseph's dream. This illustration, described on page 49, occupies the center panel of the Annunciation window found on the lectern side stairway that leads to the balcony.

TABLE OF CONTENTS

The Scripture quotations embedded within the windows of Myers Park Presbyterian Church are from the *King James Version.* Therefore the *King James Version* is used for each page which explains an overall window. All additional Scripture comes from the *New Revised Standard Version* unless otherwise noted.

Dedicated to the glory of God
and to the past, present, and future
members of Myers Park Presbyterian Church

FOREWORD

Everybody loves a good story. The Bible is a story about God's love for us. When I was a child, I not only enjoyed listening to stories, but I also liked to look at the pictures. Somehow the pictures made the story come to life. The stained glass windows in our Sanctuary make the story of God's love come to life for us.

Dr. Fred Craddock is one of my favorite preachers. He once told the story of being a small boy and attending Sunday School. He said there was no classroom for his age group, they didn't have a teacher, and there was no curriculum. They met in a small storage area until other arrangements could be made. In the room was a coffee table with a Bible story book that was illustrated with pictures. There was a picture of Jesus walking on water, a picture of the feeding of the 5,000, a picture of the crucifixion, and so forth.

Dr. Craddock said that he would flip through that picture book every Sunday morning looking at the pictures of the Bible stories and to this day, as an adult, a teacher of Greek, New Testament, and preaching, when someone mentions one of those stories, the pictures in that book pop up on the screen of his mind.

Stained glass windows are pretty, but they are also functional. As we worship, we are surrounded by the story of God's grace from Genesis through Revelation. This book helps us to get the pictures on the screen of our minds. This book helps us to study the windows and to therefore study the love of God poured out for us.

The needlepoint, linens, and other sanctuary art, much of it crafted by our own church members, serve to put the symbols of our faith on the screen of our minds. These symbols cross our lives in some of our most memorable worship experiences such as weddings, baptisms, and communion.

We are extremely grateful to all of those who have labored to give us this book of pictures. We are grateful for the people who generously contributed and gave the gift of our stained-glass windows. Above all, we are extremely grateful to God, who gave us the story of grace that is woven into the very fabric of who we are. For the pictures that come up on the screen of our mind, of how God has continually been at work redeeming us, sustaining us, forgiving us, healing us, and loving us, we give thanks.

Sit back and flip through this book of pictures with appreciation and thanks for the wonderful grace of God and for the story that we all share.

Gratefully,

Dr. Steven P. Eason

5

INTRODUCTION

Art is often both beautiful and functional; this is particularly true in the sanctuary art of churches. For centuries the symbols and illustrations of Biblical stories have both instructed and inspired the learned and the illiterate. Today in our sanctuary these same symbols, whether they appear in the colorful glass of the windows, in the delicate needlepoint stitching of the cushions and palls, or in the substantive carvings of solid oak, both beautify the sanctuary for the worship of God and instruct worshippers in the stories and truths of the Christian faith. While this book is strictly confined to the sanctuary art of Myers Park Presbyterian Church, the symbols explained here, or variations of them, have been used in religious art throughout the centuries.

Much of the art in our sanctuary is constantly available to inspire and instruct us, while other artistic elements are used less frequently - in monthly communion or in baptisms. Other pieces are confined to more private moments of worship, such as weddings and funerals. However, the entirety of the sanctuary art can both inspire us with its beauty and teach us, if we will but pay attention to what is there before our eyes.

The color and symbols of the liturgical calendar dictate many of the choices regarding the use of the sanctuary art, while the stained glass windows derive their pattern and much of their meaning from the iconography determined before the first windows were ever designed. The overall theme of the stained glass windows, developed by Henry Willet of Willet Stained Glass Studios in Philadelphia in conjunction with a committee of Myers Park Presbyterian Church members under the leadership of the Reverend Doctor James Fogartie, is "the sovereignty of God in Creation, Redemption, and History." The windows are strictly Biblical, which was always part of the intended plan. Marguerite Gaudin, of Willet Stained Glass Studios, designed each of the sixteen nave windows as well as the Chancel and Christmas windows.

The windows take a mostly chronological path through the Bible by moving in a clockwise direction around the sanctuary. Creation, as the first of the nave windows, appears as the first window near the Chancel on the lectern side. It and the next six windows present scenes from the Old Testament. The last window on this side, Preparation for the Messiah, provides a bridge between the Old Testament and the New by depicting both the last of the Old Testament prophets and John the Baptist. The three small gallery windows in the stairwell to the balcony, on the lectern side, portray the Annunciation. The large Christmas window in the balcony, also known as both the rose window and the great façade window, is the easiest to recognize. Descending the stairs on the pulpit side are three small windows portraying the childhood of Jesus. The remainder of the New Testament windows begin on the main floor near the balcony and proceed toward the pulpit. Themes in these eight windows include Jesus' baptism and calling of the disciples, the teaching, preaching, and healing ministries of Jesus, Jesus' Passion, Pentecost, and the life and ministry of Paul. The last New Testament window, the window nearest the pulpit, presents scenes from the book of the Revelation.

The central visual and spiritual focus in the sanctuary, offsetting the Christmas window and facing it, is the Chancel window, or reredos. It gloriously illustrates the theme of God's sovereignty by portraying Jesus Christ's resurrection and ascension. This window is unique among the stained glass windows of Myers Park Presbyterian Church, as it is actually panels of stained glass behind a lead-sculptured overlay, flown with 23-karat gold leaf. This construction allows the window to be lit from behind or to stand in black and gold relief.

While the overall story of God's sovereignty in creation, redemption, and history follows a carefully calculated arrangement, individually the windows do not follow a uniform pattern. The stories within each of the windows proceed in a variety of ways. Each window must be studied according to its own design; there is no order that applies to all of the windows. Instead, artistic and thematic considerations determined the arrangement of the images within each individual window. While this presents a greater challenge in following the narrative of each window, it also creates the greatest possible visual and textual interest.

The chapel windows are not included in the book, as they fall outside of the sanctuary. However, they also were created and installed by Willet Stained Glass Studios and were designed by Colum Sharkey, the designer of the sanctuary gallery windows. The central window of the chapel illustrates Psalm 148 while three pairs of side windows reflect faith, hope, and charity. The symbols used in the side windows are illuminated by Scripture references within the windows themselves.

Myers Park Presbyterian Church made a commitment in 1961, at the outset of efforts to beautify the sanctuary by means of stained glass windows, not to list or in any way publicly recognize the donors of the individual stained glass windows or the persons memorialized. Likewise, this book makes no attempt to recognize the individual members of the Take My Hands Circle, who created most of the needlework; the tireless hands that have ironed the linens and polished the silver of the sanctuary; or the donors of the individual pieces of art. Indeed the sanctuary is home to us all, and the proper intent of all it contains, including us, is to glorify God.

Kim Stump

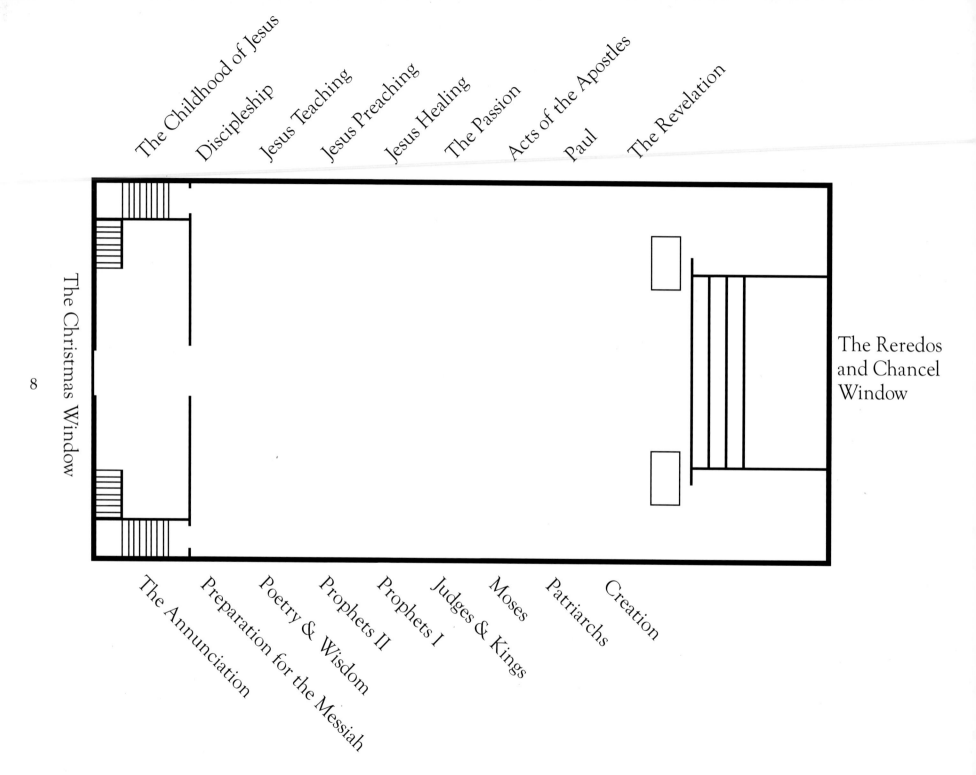

The Childhood of Jesus

Discipleship

Jesus Teaching

Jesus Preaching

Jesus Healing

The Passion

Acts of the Apostles

Paul

The Revelation

The Christmas Window

8

The Reredos
and Chancel
Window

The Annunciation

Preparation for the Messiah

Poetry & Wisdom

Prophets II

Prophets I

Judges & Kings

Moses

Patriarchs

Creation

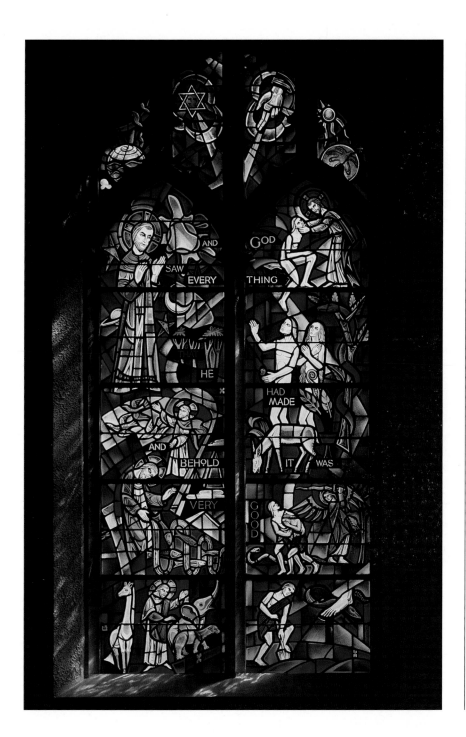

CREATION

*And God saw every thing that he had made, and,
behold, it was very good.*
Genesis 1:31a

The first window summarizes the stories of
creation. Across the top, the tracery presents symbols of
God's creation of heaven and earth. The lower portion of
the window presents the creation stories in more detail.
The left lancet shows God creating everything prior to the
creation of man and woman. Light, the heavenly bodies,
the land and sea, vegetation, sea animals, birds, and land
animals – all are made by God and pronounced "good."
The right lancet depicts God's relationship with humankind as our Creator, Judge, and Redeemer.

These symbols and vignettes emphasize God's role as the
Creator and Ruler of all things. Although made in God's
image, we are only a part of God's creation, and our
purpose and meaning come not from ourselves, but from
our Maker.

9

In the beginning when God… Genesis 1:1a

The tracery summarizes the creation in symbols. The *Manus Dei*, or hand of God, shown in the third panel, symbolizes that creation came from God. The three outstretched digits of the hand, the two fingers and the thumb, represent the Holy Trinity, while the general position of the hand is one of blessing. These symbols are particularly appropriate here, because Scripture indicates that creation was a Trinitarian endeavor (Genesis 1:1-2, 1:26, and John 1:1-4), and because the first chapter of Genesis tells of God's first blessings on parts of his creation (Genesis 1:22, 1:28). The two fingers folded into the palm symbolize the dual nature of Jesus Christ as both fully human and fully God (Hebrews 2:14-18, John 1:1-4, 1:14, 10:30). (Genesis 1:1)

10

created… Genesis 1:1a

The Creator's star (in the second panel of the tracery) is formed of interlocking triangles which symbolize the Triune God. Inside the star are two *yods*, Hebrew consonants, with vowel pointers, which represent God's name, "YHWH", meaning the Self-Existent or Eternal One. (Genesis 1:1)

the heavens and the earth,… Genesis 1:1b

The far right panel presents the sun and a globe. With the *Manus Dei* and the Creator's star, these symbols beautifully present the first verse of Scripture, focusing primarily on the Triune God, and secondarily on creation. (Genesis 1:1)

the earth was a formless void and darkness covered the face of the deep, while a wind from God swept over the face of the waters. Genesis 2:2

The far left tracery shows the earth with bands of green around it. This could be symbolic of the spirit from God; or since green is a liturgical color symbolic of growth and life, it could be the artist's imagery for the coming creation of life on earth. (Genesis 1:2)

And God said, "Let there be lights in the dome of the sky to separate the day from the night; …" Genesis 1:14a

In the top of the left lancet, God creates light and the moon, planets, and stars. The earth is shown producing vegetation. In each of the first four days of creation, God both creates and separates. God's spread hands remind us not only of the creative power of God but also of the separation and order God brings to the different parts of creation.

This figure of God also provides an excellent example of a tri-radiant (or cruciform) nimbus, the halo around God's head with three rays within. Another tri-radiant nimbus appears in the tracery around the hand of God. This symbolic design is appropriate only for the three members of the Trinity: Father, Son, or Holy Spirit. The windows of Myers Park Presbyterian Church include numerous examples of this image. (Genesis 1:3-19)

And God said, "Let the waters bring forth swarms of living creatures, …"
Genesis 1:20a

The center of the left lancet shows God on the fifth day creating the fish to swim in the water. The serpentine wave, representing the water teeming with fish, also appears in the chancel window and there represents the waters of baptism. (Genesis 1:20-23)

and let birds fly above the earth across the dome of the sky."
Genesis 1:20b

Just above the image of the seas and fish, God creates and frees the birds of the air. This fifth day presents the first record of God blessing a part of his creation. The blessing gives the birds and sea life a purpose, directing them to "be fruitful and multiply." (Genesis 1:20-23)

God made the wild animals of the earth of every kind, and the cattle of every kind, and everything that creeps upon the ground of every kind.
Genesis 1:25a

The bottom of the left lancet shows God creating land animals on the sixth day. Shown here are a giraffe, an elephant, and a bear.

As in the illustration of God creating the birds, God's hands signal the sending forth of the animals just created. (Genesis 1:24-25)

Then the Lord God formed man from the dust of the ground, and breathed into his nostrils the breath of life; and the man became a living being.
Genesis 2:7

The final pictorial of the sixth day begins at the top of the right lancet, showing God raising man from the ground. God's human appearance throughout the window emphasizes God's choice to "make man in Our image, according to Our likeness." (Genesis 1:26)

In Genesis 1:28, we see the second incidence of God blessing a portion of creation. This time the blessing falls upon the man and the woman. As in the blessing of the animals, God calls upon them to "be fruitful and multiply." But the directive to man and woman is expanded and includes the order to fill the earth and subdue it, and to rule over all the living things on earth. Genesis 2:15 also makes clear that from the very beginning Adam had work to do — the cultivating and keeping of the garden. (Genesis 1:26-2:8)

The man said, "The woman whom you gave to be with me, she gave me fruit from the tree, and I ate."
Genesis 3:12

In the center of the right lancet, Adam looks up towards an invisible God. His left hand holds a piece

11

of bitten fruit. Eve covers herself behind Adam, while the serpent, depicted in red, curls around the tree of the knowledge of good and evil. The forbidden fruit most often appears as an apple in art, as it does here. This probably developed because of the identical spelling of the Latin words for evil (*malum*) and apple (*malum*). The only difference lies in the pronunciation of the two words.

It is possible that the small animal grazing in the lower foreground is a unicorn.

As one closely examines the *lumiere*, the line drawing of the window's details made by the artist, what at first seems to be the right ear appears instead to be a horn. In the finished window, the horn appears to have whorls, as one would expect on a unicorn's horn. The unicorn is considered to be a symbol of the incarnation and the sinless life of Jesus Christ. With this interpretation, the unicorn image foreshadows the ultimate redemption of mankind as provided by God through Jesus Christ. (Genesis 2:9-3:13)

"I will put enmity between you and the woman, and between your offspring and hers; he will strike your head, and you will strike his heel."
Genesis 3:15

The heel of a human foot crushes a serpent's head in the bottom right

lancet. Ultimately Jesus Christ, a descendant of the first man and woman, will conquer sin and death, fulfilling this prophetic dictate. (Genesis 3:14-16)

He drove out the man; and at the east of the garden of Eden he placed the cherubim, and a sword flaming and turning to guard the way to the tree of life. Genesis 3:24

Adam and Eve had sought to become equal with God by eating the forbidden fruit; now God asserts almighty sovereignty over the earth and humankind by sending an angel to drive fallen man and woman from the garden and prevent their return. According to Scripture, God clothes them both in animal skins before casting them out of the garden. Scripturally incorrect, although artistically typical, this pictorial shows them fleeing the garden wearing leaves. (Genesis 3:22-24)

Therefore the Lord God sent him forth from the garden of Eden, to till the ground from which he was taken.
Genesis 3:23

Adam works the cursed land with a shovel. Although clothed in animal skins provided by God, he can no longer eat freely of the garden's fruit but must struggle in hard labor to grow enough to eat. (Genesis 3:17-24)

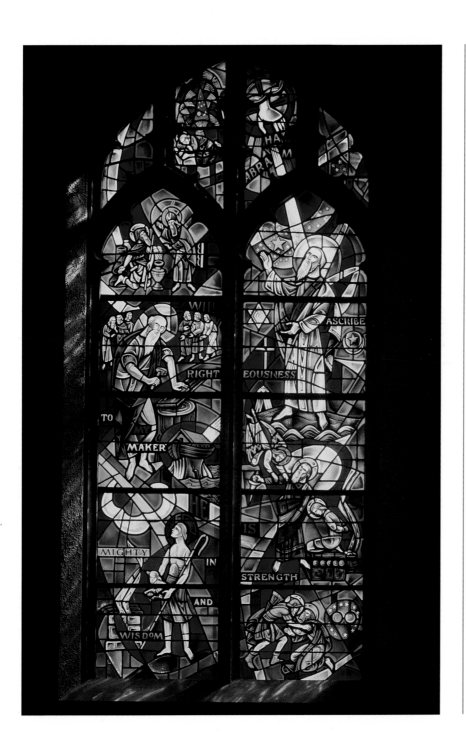

PATRIARCHS

I ... will ascribe righteousness to my Maker.
He is mighty in strength and wisdom.
Job 36:3b & 5b

The patriarchs of the faith portrayed in this window are among those enumerated in Hebrews 11, each praised for his faith. Abel, in the bottom left lancet, offers to God an acceptable sacrifice by faith. Noah, by faith in God, becomes an heir to righteousness by obediently building an ark as God commands. At the top of both lancets is Abraham, who obeys God's call to leave his homeland to go where God calls him. By faith Abraham is also willing to offer his son, Isaac, at the command of God, as the ultimate test of his faith in the Lord. This sacrifice, interrupted by the angel of the Lord, serves as a foreshadowing of the coming sacrifice of Jesus Christ, God's only Son. Esau, Jacob, and Joseph, all mentioned in the ranks of the faithful, are shown in the window. Hebrews clearly states that it is through this faith that they gain God's approval and are considered righteous.

The verse in the window is taken from the book of Job. This is quite appropriate since most likely the book of Job was set in the time period of Abraham. Additionally, using Job is in keeping with the window's theme of faith. Although Job suffers loss and vile illness, he is still able to proclaim his belief in God, saying, "For I know that my Redeemer lives, and that at the last he will stand upon the earth." (Job 19:25)

13

And Abel for his part brought of the firstlings of his flock, their fat portions.
Genesis 4:4a

Abel, the second of Adam and Eve's sons, brings a sacrifice pleasing to the Lord. Standing in front of a smoking altar, Abel holds a lamb, ready for offering. Abel's sacrifice, which he offers in faith, is the first and best of what he has and finds favor in the sight of God. In contrast, Cain, Abel's older brother, earlier brought an offering that was not acceptable to God. Although God encourages Cain to do good and master the sin prowling so near, Cain instead turns his hand against Abel and murders him.
(Genesis 4:1-16)

"Make yourself an ark of cypress wood; make rooms in the ark, and cover it inside and out with pitch."
Genesis 6:14

Because of the wickedness, corruption, violence, and evil thoughts and intentions of humankind, God intends to destroy the creatures of the earth. However, Noah, a righteous and blameless man of that generation, finds favor with God. When God instructs Noah to build an ark in preparation for a great flood, Noah obeys in faith. Not only Noah and his wife, but also Noah's three sons, depicted by the three men pictured on the right in this vignette, and their families are to be spared.

The inset of the ark shows it resting on the mountain of Ararat as the waters finally recede some five months after the flood. The arc of white light hints at the covenant God will soon make with Noah.
(Genesis 6:5-9:18)

And Abram gave [King Melchizedek of Salem] one tenth of everything.
Genesis 14:20b

As Abram returns from rescuing Lot and all the goods and people captured by an alliance of four invading kings, Melchizedek, the king and priest of Salem, meets him. This is the first instance of tithing in Scripture. Abram gives this priest-king one tenth of everything. Melchizedek literally means "king of right or righteousness" and Salem means "peace." Later, in the New Testament, Jesus' priesthood is spoken of as similar to that of Melchizedek, making Melchizedek a type of Christ figure.
(Genesis 14:11-24, Hebrews 6:19-7:17)

14

"No longer shall your name be Abram, but your name shall be Abraham; for I have made you the ancestor of a multitude of nations."
Genesis 17:5

This vignette of Abram dominates the window and portrays God Almighty changing Abram's name. God changes Abram, meaning "high or exalted father," to Abraham, meaning "father of a large multitude." The hand of God, shown in the tracery, inserts the letters HA into Abram's name. At this time God also changes the name of Abram's wife, Sarai, to Sarah, which means "princess."

During this conversation God makes a covenant with Abraham and his descendants after him, concluding with God's covenant command of male circumcision.

The tent in the lower left symbolizes the calling out of Abraham from his home and the promise of the land of Canaan as a perpetual home for his descendants.

The six-pointed star of Judaism, the cross of Christianity, and the star and crescent of Islam represent Abraham's position of father to all three religions: Judaism and Christianity claim the lineage of Abraham through Isaac, the son of Abraham and Sarah. Islam considers Abraham its patriarch through Ishmael, the son of Abram and Hagar, Sarah's maid.

The scattering of stars across the sky calls to mind the Lord's promise that Abraham's offspring would be as numerous as the stars, while the sand he stands on reminds us of the similar promise that they would be as numerous as the dust of the earth and the sands upon the seashore. The large five-pointed star in the sky is representative of the coming Messiah, Jesus Christ, the one of Abraham's descendants through whom all the nations on the earth are blessed. (Genesis 12:1-3, 13:14-18, 15:1-6, 16:1-16, 17:1-27, 22:17-18)

Then Abraham reached out his hand and took the knife to kill his son. But the angel of the Lord called to him from heaven, and said, "Abraham, Abraham!"
Genesis 22:10-11a

In God's testing of Abraham's faith, Abraham is commanded to make a sacrifice of Isaac, his son, whom he loves. In obedience Abraham makes the three-day journey with Isaac and two servants. Abraham builds the altar and puts Isaac upon it. However, before Abraham can lift the knife to his son the angel of the Lord calls out to him and stops him from harming the boy.

In this way Abraham proves his faith and obedience. In return, the Lord reiterates His covenant promise to Abraham. (Genesis 22:1-19)

[Jacob] himself went on ahead of them, bowing himself to the ground seven times, until he came near his brother. But Esau ran to meet him, and embraced him, …
Genesis 33:3-4a

Jacob and Esau, the twin sons of Isaac, greet one another after Jacob's long absence. Because Jacob cheated Esau, the first born, out of both the birthright and paternal blessing that rightfully belonged to him, Jacob is unsure how Esau will react to his return. Therefore Jacob humbles himself before Esau by bowing, not once, but seven times.

The twelve stars surrounding the sun and moon represent the twelve sons of Jacob, who will eventually become the foundation of the twelve tribes of Israel. (Genesis 32:1-33:20)

[Joseph] had another dream, and told it to his brothers, saying, "Look, I have had another dream: the sun, the moon, and eleven stars were bowing down to me."
Genesis 37:9

Joseph, Rachel's firstborn and Jacob's favorite, has two prophetic dreams while still a teenager. He first dreams of eleven sheaves of wheat bowing down before his own. This causes his older brothers considerable consternation, as they fear he might someday have authority over them. The second dream, of eleven stars, the sun, and the moon bowing down before Joseph, takes even Jacob aback. Jacob interprets the dream to mean his sons, his wife and even he would bow before Joseph. Therefore, he rebukes Joseph. (Genesis 37:1-11)

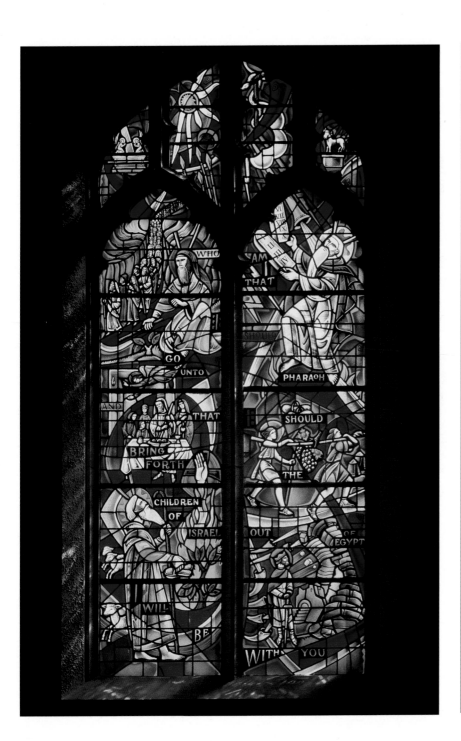

MOSES

Who am I, that I should go unto Pharaoh, and that I should bring forth the children of Israel out of Egypt? …I will be with [you;]
Exodus 3:11b & 3:12a

This window focuses on God's faithfulness as Moses leads the people of Israel. The window begins with God's speaking to Moses from the burning bush. During this exchange Moses asks God in trepidation, "Who am I that I should go unto Pharaoh, and that I should bring forth the children of Israel out of Egypt?" God's answer, as it so frequently does, focuses not on Moses or any special attributes that might make Moses worthy or able to do this great and impossible thing but rather on God Almighty, the Great I Am. God responds, "I will be with you." Ultimately, Moses discovers that God's presence is indeed enough.

In the tracery, God demonstrates his presence by the pillar of fire and cloud that leads the Israelites. The tracery portrays the Ark of the Covenant, where God talks to Moses. Directly opposite is the statue of the golden calf, made by Aaron in disobedience to God's commands.

The left lancet contains both the keeping of the Passover, so the destroyer does not touch the first-born, and the Israelites walking through the Red Sea. Both the receiving of the Ten Commandments and the return of the spies from the Promised Land, in the right lancet, reflect God's faithfulness. The final illustration of the window shows Joshua standing before the crumbling walls of Jericho.

17

When the Lord saw that he had turned aside to see, God called to him out of the bush, "Moses, Moses!" And he said, "Here I am." Then he said, "Come no closer! Remove the sandals from your feet, for the place on which you are standing is holy ground." Exodus 3:4-5

As Moses tends his father-in-law's sheep, he passes through the wilderness to Mount Horeb. There, Moses encounters the Living God, who speaks to him out of a burning bush. In the window, flames flicker above and around the bush as the hand of God extends above it. Moses holds his sandals in one hand, in obedience to God's command, and his staff in the other. The staff reflects Moses' position as a shepherd, as do the scampering sheep. The staff also reminds us of one of the signs that God will give Moses to convince Pharaoh to let the Israelites go that they might worship God.

During this talk with God, Moses asks, "Who am I that I should go unto Pharaoh, and that I should bring forth the children of Israel out of Egypt?" God's response expresses his sovereignty: "Certainly I will be with you." It will not be Moses who accomplishes the ultimate release of his people from Pharaoh but the power of God working through him.

The window portrays Moses in the traditional style, with two "horns" or rays emanating from his head. Here they appear as blue rays projecting through the nimbus, or halo, around Moses' head. This image originated from an early translation of the Hebrew text to Latin of the verses in Exodus 34. The Hebrew word that we now translate "shone" was translated into a phrase meaning "to shoot out horns." (In fact, the famous sculpture of Moses by Michelangelo bears what appear to be actual horns.) (Exodus 3:1-4:23)

This is how you shall eat it: your loins girded, your sandals on your feet, and your staff in your hand; and you shall eat it hurriedly. It is the passover of the Lord ... The blood shall be a sign for you on the houses where you live: when I see the blood, I will pass over you, and no plague shall destroy you when I strike the land of Egypt. Exodus 12:11 & 13

An Israelite family gathers together in obedience to God's command, staff in the father's hand, sandals on their feet, to eat the Passover meal. Above them flies the destroyer, passing by the door whose lintel is marked with the blood of the Passover lamb. Where the doors are not marked in blood, the firstborn will die. Thus God saves faithful Israelites from this plague of death; but the Egyptians, with doors unmarked, lose their firstborn. It is this sign from God that finally leads Pharaoh to drive the Israelites out of Egypt. (Exodus 11:1-12:33)

18

The Lord went in front of them in a pillar of cloud by day, to lead them along the way, and in a pillar of fire by night, to give them light, so that they might travel by day and by night.
Exodus 13:21

The tracery shows symbols of the Israelites' escape from Egypt. The sun and the moon, in conjunction with the red and white columns of fire and clouds, symbolize the constant presence of the Lord as the Israelites flee.

By day, God goes before them in a pillar of cloud; by night, God leads them from within a pillar of fire. In this way the Israelites are able to travel day and night. The upright spears represent the pursuing Egyptian army. (Exodus 13:17-14:11)

Then Moses stretched out his hand over the sea. The Lord drove the sea back by a strong east wind all night, and turned the sea into dry land; and the waters were divided. The Israelites went into the sea on dry ground, the waters forming a wall for them on their right and on their left.
Exodus 14:21-22

The Israelites, fearing that the pursuing Egyptian army will overtake and kill them, cry out in desperation to Moses. Moses encourages them that God will fight for them while they remain silent. God commands Moses to send the people onward toward the sea and to stretch out his staff to part the water.

Moses and the people obey. Within the pillar of cloud and fire, the angel of God alone stands between them and the Egyptians. The people pass safely out of Egypt and the Egyptian army is destroyed. As a result, the Israelites fear the Lord and put their trust in God and his servant Moses. (Exodus 14:10-31)

When God finished speaking with Moses on Mount Sinai, he gave him the two tablets of the covenant, tablets of stone, written with the finger of God.
Exodus 31:18

Three months after the Israelites' escape from Egypt, God descends upon Mount Sinai in fire, accompanied by the sounds of thunder and trumpet and the sight of lightning and clouds. It is here that God calls Moses to the top of the mountain and verbally gives the Ten Commandments and other ordinances to Moses, for him to deliver to the people. All the people agree to abide by the Lord's words and commands, and Moses writes down the Lord's words for them.

It is only at this point that Moses, with his servant Joshua, returns to the top of the mountain to receive from the Lord the actual stone tablets of the Law, which God writes for the instruction of the people. To the people remaining below, the appearance of the

19

glory of God is like a consuming fire on the mountaintop, represented by the fire at Moses' feet. The lightning bolts and the trumpet blast are also represented in this vignette.

For forty days and nights Moses remains on the mountain, receiving detailed instructions from God regarding the building of a tabernacle in which the people could worship God. At the end of this time God gives Moses the two stone tablets of the covenant.

In the window, the two tablets that Moses appears to receive from above are shown in a conventionally Calvinistic style. Representative Roman numerals depict the first four commandments on the first tablet and the latter six commandments on the second. In this division, the first four commandments explain our responsibilities to God, the remaining six our responsibilities within our families and communities. (Exodus 19-31)

There I will meet with you, and from above the mercy seat, from between the two cherubim that are on the ark of the covenant, I will deliver to you all my commands for the Israelites.
Exodus 25:22

A portion of Moses' instructions from God about the tabernacle includes the building of an ark. The ark was to contain the tablets of the covenant, which God gives to Moses; on top of the ark was to rest the mercy seat between two gold cherubim. The Lord tells Moses that it is there, where the law of the covenant and mercy symbolically come together, that the Lord will meet with Moses. (Exodus 25:1-22)

[Aaron] took the gold from them, formed it in a mold, and cast an image of a calf; and they said, "These are your gods, O Israel, who brought you up out of the land of Egypt!"
Exodus 32:4

During the time that Moses is on the mountain with God, receiving instructions for worship, the Israelite people grow impatient. They go to Aaron and implore him, in the continuing absence of Moses, to make a god for them that will go before them. Aaron succumbs to their demands; instructing the people to remove their earrings, he takes the gold and fashions it into a golden calf. The people worship and sacrifice to it, causing the anger of the Lord to burn against them. When God tells Moses, still on the mountain, what is happening, Moses intercedes for the people, pleading for God's mercy. However, when Moses returns from the mountain with the tablets of stone and sees for himself the sin of the people, he destroys the tablets in a rage. Additionally, Moses destroys the golden idol and again intercedes for the people. (Exodus 32)

And they came to the Wadi Eshcol, and cut down from there a branch with a single cluster of grapes, and they carried it on a pole between two of them.
Numbers 13:23a

At the Lord's instruction, Moses sends out twelve spies to explore Canaan, the promised land. One spy from each of the twelve tribes is chosen to go. During the forty days they explore the land, the twelve happen upon a valley with magnificent fruit: grapes, figs, and pomegranates. The grape cluster in particular

20

is so large that it is placed on a pole and carried between two of the spies back to the Israelite people.

Showing only two of the returning spies serves as a reminder that of the twelve sent, only two, Joshua and Caleb, return with confidence that the Lord will actually enable the Israelites to successfully attain the promised land. Because of their apprehension, the remaining ten spies spread exaggerated reports of the fierceness of the people currently living on the land. Fear arises within the Israelites to the point that they will not listen to Moses and his assurances that God is with them. Instead, grumbling against Moses and God, the people rebel and refuse to go in to take the land as God commands. The result is that none of that adult generation, except Joshua and Caleb, are allowed to enter Canaan. (Numbers 13:1-14:38)

And the Lord said to Moses, "Make a poisonous serpent, and set it on a pole; and everyone who is bitten shall look at it and live."
Numbers 21:8

As the Israelites wander in the wilderness, still led by God, but not yet allowed to enter Canaan, the Israelites again become impatient. In their impatience, they again grumble and rebel against God. Poisonous serpents come among the people, killing many; but at Moses' intercession the Lord makes provision so that those bitten might live. God instructs Moses to make a serpent and place it on a staff. Moses does as God

instructs and any who are bitten can look at the bronze serpent and live.

Jesus later uses this imagery to explain to Nicodemus how he would save the world. The symbol of a snake on a staff is symbolic of Jesus Christ, lifted upon a cross and crucified that we might live. This same symbol also appears in the Jesus Healing window on the New Testament side of the sanctuary. (Numbers 21:4-9, John 3:14-15)

So the people shouted, and the trumpets were blown. As soon as the people heard the sound of the trumpets, they raised a great shout, and the wall fell down flat; so the people charged straight ahead into the city and captured it.
Joshua 6:20

Joshua stands before the crumbling walls of Jericho. The outer wall of Jericho falls because Joshua leads the people as God commands. For six days the warriors of Israel silently march once around the city while seven priests bear the Ark of the Covenant and continually blow trumpets of rams' horns. On the seventh day the people silently march around the city six times; on the seventh and final circuit the trumpets blast, the people shout, and the walls collapse.

Six rams' horns are shown, each blasting forth its loud sound. Although Joshua wears what appears to be a crown, Joshua is not Israel's king but merely its leader, appointed by God following Moses' death.

21

God encourages Joshua to be strong, courageous, and obedient to all that was written by Moses. God's promise to Joshua, "The Lord your God is with you wherever you go," (Joshua 1:9b) is similar to God's promise to Moses, "I will be with you." (Exodus 3:12a) (Joshua 6)

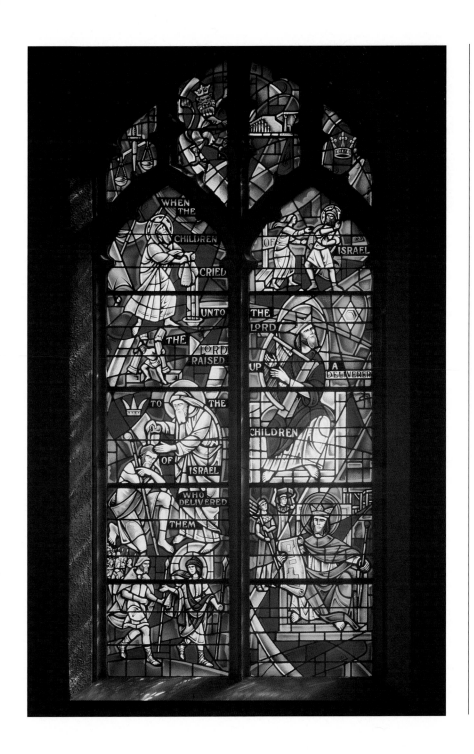

JUDGES & KINGS

….when the children of Israel cried unto the Lord, the Lord raised up a deliverer to the children of Israel, who delivered them…
Judges 3:9a

Two themes stand out from the stories portrayed in this window. The first is God's faithfulness. Although the Israelites stray from God's way time and again, serving false gods and doing evil in God's sight, God is faithful. Time after time God delivers them when they cry out to the Lord. God does this by putting the Spirit of the Lord upon certain people and appointing them judges, prophets, and kings. The second theme is a continuation of the idea of the faithful cloud of witnesses outlined in Hebrews 11. Through their individual faith in God and God's promises, these men and women are empowered to perform acts of righteousness. God uses them in spite of their weaknesses and failings because of their faith in Him.

The first of these people of faith is the judge Deborah. She directs the liberation of the Israelites from the people of Canaan in obedience to God's commands. Gideon, so fearful and insecure that he asks God not for one sign but for two, is shown wringing out a fleece. Yet God uses Gideon mightily in delivering the people from the Midianites. Jephthah rescues his people but devastates his family because of a rash vow to God. Samson battles the Philistines though he is overcome by temptation. Samuel, a judge and prophet, faithfully anoints Saul the first king of Israel. David pleases God mightily and successfully rules the people of God, but like Samson he falls into temptation. Finally, Solomon fulfills David's dream of building the temple although he later succumbs to idolatry when he fails to heed God's commands.

23

Barak summoned Zebulun and Naphtali to Kedesh; and ten thousand warriors went up behind him; and Deborah went up with him.
Judges 4:10

After Joshua dies, God appoints judges to lead the people of Israel. The fourth judge God appoints for the Israelites is Deborah. Both a wife and a mother, Deborah is a prophetess who instructs the men of Israel as they come to her for judgment.

During the time of Deborah, Jabin, the king of Canaan, oppresses the Israelites. Deborah calls for Barak, a fellow Israelite, and explains that God desires for him to lead an attack against Sisera, the commander of Jabin's army. Barak agrees but only if Deborah goes with him into battle. Hence, the first vignette in this window portrays Deborah and Barak leading a procession of Israelite soldiers. When Deborah agrees to go with him she also prophesies that since Barak was unwilling to go without her, he himself will not defeat Sisera; rather, a woman will be the victor over Jabin's commander. Indeed, the outcome is as Deborah foretold. Sisera dies at the hands of Jael, a Kenite (Midianite) woman. The death of Sisera turns the tide against the Canaanites, and after their eventual defeat the Israelites live in peace for forty years. (Judges 4-5)

When [Gideon] rose early next morning and squeezed the fleece, he wrung enough dew from the fleece to fill a bowl with water.
Judges 6:38b

Gideon is both reluctant and doubtful when the angel of the Lord first approaches him with the news that Gideon is to deliver his people from the Midianites. The Lord's assurance, as it was to Moses, is "But I will be with you..." (Judges 6:16) In a first step towards this deliverance, Gideon obeys God's order to destroy the altar of Baal and the Asherah, but Gideon is too afraid during the day and destroys them at night.

Afterwards, in order to gain confidence in God's promise to deliver the Israelites, Gideon asks for a sign. Gideon puts out a fleece, requesting that it be wet and the ground dry if God will indeed deliver Israel by Gideon's hand. Although God provides the sign requested, Gideon asks for another sign, this time that the fleece be dry and the ground wet. Once Gideon receives this second sign, he fearfully moves forward as God directs. After more conversation and direction from God aimed at alleviating Gideon's fear, the troops indeed overcome the Midianites as God promised.

Gideon serves as a wonderful reminder that God is faithful to accomplish all that is promised even when God's people are fearful and afraid. (Judges 6-8)

Then Jephthah came to his home at Mizpah; and there was his daughter coming out to meet him with timbrels and with dancing. She was his only child; he had no son or daughter except her.
Judges 11:34

Another cycle of peace followed by the worship of other gods and the subsequent oppression by foreigners occurs, and the Israelites cry out to the Lord and ask for deliverance. The elders of Gilead choose Jephthah because of his reputation as a courageous warrior. Then the Spirit of the Lord comes upon Jephthah, and the Israelites are again victorious over their adversaries.

Unfortunately, prior to the battle, Jephthah makes a rash vow to God. He promises that whatever meets him at the doors of his home on his return will be offered to God as a burnt offering. Jephthah has only one child, a daughter. Tragically, his daughter meets him as he triumphantly returns home. The vignette portrays Jephthah recoiling as his daughter eagerly runs toward him. (Judges 10:6-11:40)

And Samson grasped the two middle pillars on which the house rested, and he leaned his weight against them, his right hand on the one and his left hand on the other.
Judges 16:29

Samson's role as a judge of Israel is distinguished from other judges because Samson is appointed to deliver Israel from the Philistines even before his conception. The angel of the Lord appears to his mother and announces that Samson is to be reared as a Nazirite, one consecrated to God, from the womb.

Although Samson is chosen and empowered by God, he toys with temptation and falls into sin. This pictorial reflects the very end of Samson's life, when he again turns to God and prays for one more chance to fulfill the mission given him by God and to revenge his capture by the Philistines. God grants Samson's request. In sacrificing his life Samson delivers Israel from many of the Philistine rulers. (Judges 13-16)

Samuel took a vial of oil and poured it on his head, and kissed him; he said, "The Lord has anointed you ruler over his people Israel. You shall reign over the people of the Lord and you will save them from the hand of their enemies all around."
I Samuel 10:1a

Samuel, the Lord's prophet and a judge of Israel, stands anointing Saul as the first king of Israel. Saul, from the tribe of Benjamin, kneels. This is an accurate reflection of both Saul's modesty (at this point) and his height. Additionally, he is also handsome and from a wealthy family.

The crown sits in midair because Saul has not yet publicly been made king. Rather, God instructs Samuel to first anoint Saul privately. Samuel anoints Saul, using a vial of oil, and then openly proclaims Saul king one week later.

This event marks a clear demarcation in Israel's history. Although the Israelites had been led by Moses as well as by numerous judges, and had even pleaded with Gideon to be their king none had ever actually reigned over Israel except the Lord God Almighty. Israel's demand for a king, in order to be like the other nations around them, is a rejection of God as their king. However, God allows and even chooses this first king who will rule them.

God eventually deposes Saul, whose impatience, rebellion, and stubbornness lead him to disobey God's commands. (I Samuel 3, 7:15-10:13, 13, 15)

David was thirty years old when he began to reign, and he reigned forty years.
2 Samuel 5:4

A crowned King David sits on his throne, playing a harp. The Star of David, a symbol of modern-day Israel, is positioned in the upper right.

The prophet Samuel, who had anointed Saul, anointed David privately among his family several years before he was actually crowned the second king of Israel. At the time, David was a young man, ruddy in complexion and handsome in appearance, with beautiful eyes. As the youngest son of his father, he was the keeper of the sheep.

At David's anointing the spirit of the Lord came mightily, even as it left Saul and plunged Saul into a state of torment and apparent depression. Indeed, King Saul's emotional state first caused David to be brought to the king, that David might play for him on the harp and soothe him. David was described to Saul as a skillful musician, a warrior, and a man of valor, while being both prudent in his speech and a man of God's presence. But perhaps the most significant thing about David is that he was a man after God's own heart.

The harp points to David's talent as a musician and psalmist as well as his playing the harp for King Saul. The throne on which David sits serves as a reminder that King David captures the stronghold of Zion and establishes Jerusalem as the capital of Israel. (1 Samuel 13:14, 16:1-23; 2 Samuel 2:1-7, 5:1-25)

"Judah is a lion's whelp; from the prey, my son, you have gone up. He crouches down, he stretches out like a lion, like a lioness – who dares rouse him up? The scepter shall not depart from Judah, nor the ruler's staff from between his feet, until tribute comes to him; and the obedience of the peoples is his." Genesis 49:9-10

The lion is a symbol of King David that harkens back to the prophecy of Jacob found in Genesis. The lion is also a symbol for Jesus Christ, as he is called "the Lion of the tribe of Judah." (Revelation 5:5) In this window of the judges and kings the lion reminds us that the Messiah comes both from the tribe of Judah and from the line of David. (Genesis 49:8-12, 1 Samuel 17:34-37, 2 Samuel 7:16, Revelation 5:5)

Your house and your kingdom shall be made sure forever before me; your throne shall be established forever. 2 Samuel 7:16

The crown in the tracery is symbolic of the rank and royalty of the kings of Israel. A crown can also represent David, as well as the kingly office of Jesus Christ. This symbolism works well with the Lion of

Judah symbol also found in the tracery. (2 Samuel 7:16, Revelation 19:16)

The house that King Solomon built for the Lord was sixty cubits long, twenty cubits wide, and thirty cubits high.
1 Kings 6:2

King Solomon sits upon the throne of his father David. In one hand he holds a royal scepter, indicative of his authority as king. In the other, he holds the plans for the temple. King David had passionately desired to build a house for the Lord, but God had denied him that privilege because David was a man of war. However, God did promise David that his son Solomon would build a house for the Lord and God gave David the specific instructions for the design. In addition God promises that the throne of David will be established forever. This is fulfilled by Jesus Christ. (Luke 1:30-34, Acts 2:22-3, Revelation 21:1-9)

The structure of the temple rises in the background to the right. To the left are two workers; their clothing is atypical of that found in the rest of the windows. This is perhaps an oblique reference to the fact that the temple was built using Phoenician workers, as well as the labor of the foreigners living in Israel. (2 Samuel 7, 1 Kings 5-6, 2 Chronicles 2)

Thus all the work that Solomon did for the house of the Lord was finished.
2 Chronicles 5:1a

Both the construction of the temple building and all its furnishings are complete after seven years. Solomon dedicates the temple and the glory of the Lord fills the house of God. (1 Kings 6, 2 Chronicles 2-5)

All Israel heard of the judgment that the king had rendered; and they stood in awe of the king, because they perceived that the wisdom of God was in him, to execute justice.
1 Kings 3:28

The sword and balance are symbolic of justice. In this window they expressly refer to the sage justice of King Solomon, the result of the wise and discerning mind with which God blesses Solomon. The most famous example of Solomon's wisdom in judgment is the narrative of the two women with one dead and one living baby. Both have birthed a child, and one infant has died. One woman accuses the other of having switched the babies. When Solomon astutely discerns to whom the child actually belongs, the people of Israel are awed at Solomon's wise justice. (I Kings 3:3-28)

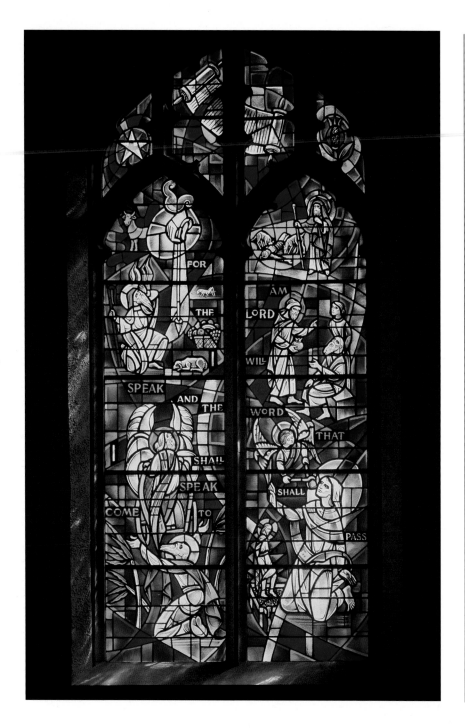

PROPHETS I

For I am the Lord: I will speak, and the word that I shall speak shall come to pass;
Ezekiel 12:25a

The two themes of this first prophets window are the surety of God's prophetic word and God's loving faithfulness in spite of his people's faithlessness. The verse in the window, from the book of Ezekiel, appropriately expresses the theme of God's commitment to fulfill the word. Elijah and Elisha, pictured in the bottom left lancet, play out God's promise of Elijah's departure and the provision made for Elisha. Above the chariot horses' heads, Amos portends the coming ruin of the northern kingdom of Israel. Although he is not taken seriously because of the affluent conditions of society, the word of the Lord nevertheless comes to pass. In the top of the right tracery, the gory end of Queen Jezebel occurs just as God said it would.

God's faithfulness in the face of the Israelites' unfaithfulness is most poignantly portrayed in the allegorical life of Hosea, as he buys back his adulterous wife, Gomer. This is shown in the middle of the right lancet. Finally, in the bottom of the right lancet is Isaiah, on his knees because of an overwhelming vision of God. Isaiah, as well as other prophets, expound on God's holiness as well as magnifying God's lovingkindness that will result in the ultimate provision of the Messiah. In the tracery a scroll represents all prophecy. A star and pomegranate flank the scroll, symbolizing two characteristics of the coming Messiah, his incarnation and his resurrection.

As they continued walking and talking, a chariot of fire and horses of fire separated the two of them, and Elijah ascended in a whirlwind into heaven.
2 Kings 2:11

Elijah, God's prophet during the reign of the wicked King Ahab and Queen Jezebel, is known for his courageous passion and his success as a prophet of God. Elijah also knows times of depression and anxiety, particularly when he is pursued and threatened by Jezebel.

The New Testament compares John's bold proclamation of God's word to that of Elijah, (Luke 1:17) and Elijah meets with Jesus and Moses during the Transfiguration (Matthew 17:1-13, Mark 9:2-13, Luke 9:28-36).

In this vignette, taken from the end of Elijah's tenure on earth, Elijah stands in the chariot of fire, pulled by horses, and gazes upward as he ascends to heaven. The bent limbs of the trees signify the accompanying whirlwind. Elisha, his servant, reaches out to him in a posture of supplication, a reminder that Elisha has asked for a double share of Elijah's spirit. God grants this, and Elisha becomes the next prophet of the God of Israel. (2 Kings 2:1-14)

When they came back and told [Jehu], he said, "This is the word of the Lord, which he spoke by his servant Elijah the Tishbite, 'In the territory of Jezreel the dogs shall eat the flesh of Jezebel;'"
2 Kings 9:36

Jezebel, the queen of Israel who was given to witchcraft, worshipping false gods, and merciless killing, lies dead in the street as dogs eat her flesh. This event fulfills a prophecy which Elijah told Jezebel's husband, King Ahab. Although by this point in the Biblical narrative Elijah has already gone to heaven in the whirlwind, the word of the Lord still comes to pass. This is a vivid example of the verse from Ezekiel inscribed in the window.

The man standing in the foreground may portray Elijah, Elisha, or Jehu. Elijah is the prophet who foretold the ignoble death of Jezebel, Elisha is the prophet of Israel during the time of her death, and Jehu is the recently anointed king of Israel who orders Jezebel's death. (1 Kings 21, 2 Kings 9:1-37)

29

This is what he showed me: the Lord was standing beside a wall built with a plumb line, with a plumb line in his hand.
Amos 7:7

Amos, a sheep herdsman and a grower of sycamore trees, is from Tekoa, a city of Judah. The shepherd's crook in his hand and the sheep lying at his feet signify his primary occupation. Among the twelve Minor Prophets the shepherd's crook represents Amos.

God calls Amos away from both his livelihood and his homeland to prophesy in the

Northern Kingdom of Israel about God's condemnation of the people's immorality, injustice, and hypocritical worship. Amos also asserts God's appeal: for the people to love and seek goodness and to establish justice. Within the region it is a time of relative peace and prosperity, making Amos's job all the more difficult.

The first vision God presents to Amos is of locusts devouring the grass of the land. Translated "grasshoppers" in the King James Version, the insect in our window more closely resembles a grasshopper than a locust. The second vision is of a judgment by fire, depicted by the flames rising from behind Amos's head and arm. The hand of God holding a plumb line among his people represents the third vision. A plumb line is symbolic of God's judgment based upon his revealed law. God's people have strayed from God's standard and fail to meet the test of the plumb line. This is the vision that dominates the window image of Amos. The fourth vision, the basket of ripe summer fruit, symbolizes that the time is at hand for Israel's judgment.

The calf in the upper left corner of this pictorial is symbolic of the fifth and final vision of Amos. About 200 years before Amos, King Jeroboam I created two golden calves and commanded worship of them for the northern tribes of Israel. Jeroboam I feared losing his power to the King of Judah if the people were allowed to worship in Jerusalem. The calves were placed in Bethel, which was on the way to Jerusalem, and in Dan, which was the northernmost part of the kingdom (1 Kings 12:25-33). This calf worship is an example of the type of false worship still going on during the time of Amos. In fact, the fifth vision of Amos reveals God standing by the idolatrous altar condemning all but a remnant of the Israelites. (Amos 7-9)

The Lord said to me again, "Go, love a woman who has a lover and is an adulteress, just as the Lord loves the people of Israel, though they turn to other gods and love raisin cakes." So I bought her for fifteen shekels of silver and a homer of barley and a measure of wine.
Hosea 3:1-2

Hosea, a contemporary of Amos, begins to prophesy several years after Amos. While Amos foretells the judgment of God and the end of the prosperity of the northern kingdom, Hosea prophesies to a northern kingdom that is now in turmoil and need.

God calls Hosea to marry, love, and rear children with a prostitute to provide a living allegory to the people of Israel of both their spiritual adultery and God's love. Obediently, Hosea marries Gomer.

God's people, the Israelites, are condemned by God through the prophet Hosea for their idolatry, wickedness, and violence. Throughout the book God calls the people to repentance and back to relationship, promising healing and love.

The illustration within our window is of the pivotal scene within the book of Hosea. Hosea buys his wife, Gomer, back from the one with whom she has been committing adultery. Although Gomer is already his wife, it is necessary for Hosea to redeem her because of her behavior. In this case it requires silver, barley, and wine. Just so, the Lord God promises that the people of God will be betrothed to the Lord in righteousness and justice, as well as in loving kindness and compassion, paying whatever price is necessary to bring us back. (Hosea 2-3)

30

Then one of the seraphs flew to me, holding a live coal that had been taken from the altar with a pair of tongs.
Isaiah 6:6

Isaiah's visions come during the same time period as Hosea's. Like Hosea, Isaiah chastises the Israelites for their iniquity, evil, corruption, and rebellion against the Holy One of Israel.

The sixth chapter of Isaiah is depicted in our windows. In the year 740 B.C., the year of King Uzziah's death, Isaiah has a vision of the King of kings, God Almighty, sitting on a throne with his robe filling the temple. Isaiah sees seraphim, creatures with six wings who are able to fly and stand and speak, above the throne. As they call to one another, "Holy, holy, holy is the Lord of hosts; the whole earth is full of his glory," the thresholds tremble and the temple fills with smoke.

Isaiah cries out in fear and voices his trepidation at being a man of unclean lips among a people of unclean lips that has seen the King, the Lord of hosts. It is at this point that one of the seraphs flies to Isaiah with a burning coal from the altar and touches Isaiah's lips. With that symbolic act of cleansing, God asks who might be sent for the purposes of the Divine. Isaiah volunteers, saying, "Here am I. Send me!" (Isaiah 6)

"It is I, announcing vindication, mighty to save. I have trodden the wine press alone, and from the peoples no one was with me;"
Isaiah 63:1c & 3a

Since the book of Isaiah holds over thirty Messianic prophecies, it is fitting that one should be highlighted alongside the prophet Isaiah. This particular illustration portrays the prophecy of the Messiah treading the wine press of God's wrath. (Isaiah 63, Revelation 14:19)

"And the Lord said to me, 'Go, prophesy to my people Israel.'"
Amos 7:15b

31

This scroll in the center of the tracery signifies all prophecy. In the Old Testament true prophets of God at times foretold future events. However, prophecy also has the much broader connotation of obediently speaking the authentic word of God.

"I see him, but not now; I behold him, but not near - a star shall come out of Jacob, and a scepter shall rise out of Israel;"
Numbers 24:17a
"Where is the child who has been born king of the Jews? For we observed his star at its rising, and have come to pay him homage."
Matthew 2:2

The five-pointed star is used to symbolize either the Incarnation or the Epiphany of Jesus Christ. The star appears in the tracery of this window because of the frequent Messianic prophecies within the Old Testament, prophecies which reach their fulfillment in the birth and life of Jesus Christ.
(Numbers 24:17, Jeremiah 23:5, Matthew 2:2)

To this day I have had help from God, and so I stand here, testifying to both small and great, saying nothing but what the prophets and Moses said would take place: that the Messiah must suffer, and that, by being the first to rise from the dead, he would proclaim light both to our people and to the Gentiles."
Acts 26:22-23

While the star is representative of the birth of Jesus and the revelation of the Messiah to humanity, the bursting pomegranate signifies the resurrection of Jesus and the promised resurrection of believers. The pomegranate stands open as the tomb was open. Additionally, the many seeds of the pomegranate are symbolic of the many people that will be resurrected as faithful followers of Christ. (Acts 26:22-23, I Corinthians 15)

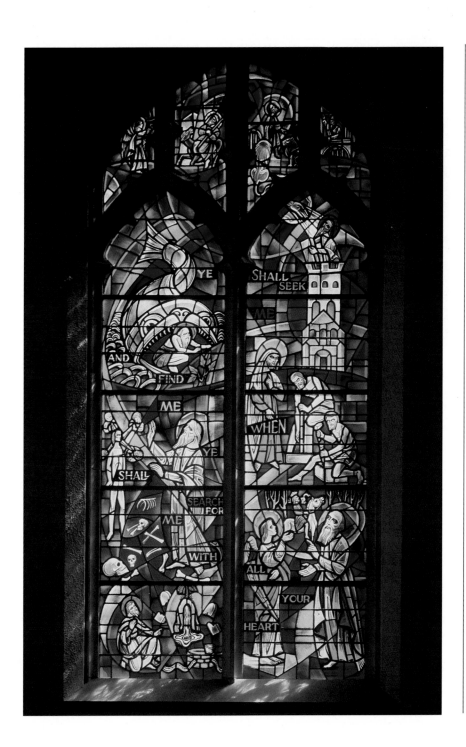

PROPHETS II

...ye shall seek me, and find me, when ye shall search for me with all your heart.
Jeremiah 29:13

In this verse from the book of Jeremiah, God speaks words of promise to the people who wholeheartedly search for the Lord. In Balaam, visible in the left tracery, we have an example of one who is definitely divided in heart; and in Daniel, visible in the right tracery, we have a wonderful example of one who commits to seeking God first and foremost.

Jonah, crouching in the mouth of the fish in the top of the left lancet, attempts to escape God and pays a most interesting price. Habakkuk, just opposite Jonah, stands on the watchtower and serves as a superb representative of those who genuinely seek the Lord for answers to the hard questions in life.

Back in the left lancet Ezekiel appears in the valley of the dry bones; below him is Jeremiah, among the broken cisterns and tablets of the law. These images figuratively illustrate what happens when God is forsaken. However, at the same time, in Ezekiel's vignette living breath flows into the dead body, while Jeremiah kneels by the fountain of living water. Both of these life-giving symbols serve to characterize God's provision of abundant life for those who seek the Lord.

The final two illustrations are of Haggai and Zechariah and appear in the right lancet. They are examples of God's encouragement to the people. These prophets reflect the Lord of hosts' continuing desire for the people to search for and find Almighty God, that they may be comforted and have peace.

33

Then the Lord opened the eyes of Balaam, and he saw the angel of the Lord standing in the road, with his drawn sword in his hand; and he bowed down, falling on his face.
Numbers 22:31

During the time of Moses, after conquering both the Amorites and the king of Bashan, the Israelites camp on the outskirts of Moab. The king of Moab, fearing invasion by the Israelites, summons Balaam, a seer. The king demands that Balaam come and curse the Israelites. Eventually, God allows Balaam to depart for Moab, with the restriction that Balaam do only as the Lord commands. Balaam soon angers God by some perverse behavior, so God places the angel of the Lord before the ass on which Balaam rides. Three times the donkey balks at the sight of the sword-wielding angel of the Lord, and each time Balaam beats her. At the third beating, the Lord permits the donkey to speak and then opens Balaam's eyes that he might also see and hear the angel of the Lord. The angel of the Lord rebukes Balaam for his behavior, and strictly commands him to speak only those words given him by God. Once Balaam arrives in Moab he is obedient to God. As a result of Balaam's obedience, the Israelites, instead of being cursed, are thrice blessed by God through the words Balaam proclaims. (Numbers 22-24)

34

Then the Lord spoke to the fish, and it spewed Jonah out upon the dry land.
Jonah 2:10

Jonah's call to Nineveh occurs during the reign of King Jeroboam II, placing Jonah in his position as reluctant prophet during roughly the same time frame as both Hosea and Amos. At this time, Nineveh was the capital city of Assyria, and the Assyrian army posed a threat to Israel. Called by God to go preach repentance in this wicked and pagan city, Jonah attempts to flee from the presence of the Lord. Jonah tries to get as far from Nineveh as possible and takes the first available ship to Tarshish.

When a great storm erupts at sea, Jonah confesses that he is running from God and offers to be thrown overboard. The sailors throw him over, but he does not drown. Instead, God sends a great fish to swallow Jonah. In this bizarre and desperate situation as a captive in the belly of a great fish, Jonah repents of his disobedience and agrees to go and prophesy to the city of Nineveh. Disgorged upon land, Jonah dutifully sets out for Nineveh; when he arrives he prophesies the coming judgment of God. The people of Nineveh, as well as their king, take Jonah's proclamations to heart and repent with fasting and prayer. Mercifully, God relents from the destruction Jonah has been predicting.

Jonah, however, is not pleased about this. Rather, he is angry and resentful that God has spared the people of Nineveh. Jonah leaves the city, sulking as he does so.

The small green plant in the foreground of this illustration is a reminder of the plant that God grows for Jonah's comfort as he sits alone outside the city and that God then causes to wither. Although Jonah is furious with God for this, God remains in conversation with Jonah, encouraging him to see the need for compassion and the reality of God's mercy on all of creation. (Jonah 1-4)

I will stand at my watchpost, and station myself on the rampart; I will keep watch to see what he will say to me, and what he will answer concerning my complaint.
Habakkuk 2:1

Habakkuk, most likely living during the time of the evil King Jehoiakim of Israel, fervently questions God on the timeless mystery of why evil exists. Soon, the Babylonians will deport Jerusalem's best leaders into slavery, but for now Habakkuk sees only the present dangers: violence, lawlessness, and perverted justice. He brings these grievances to his God.

The illustration portrays Habakkuk standing on his rampart watching and waiting for God to answer. God instructs him to write on a tablet, seen in Habakkuk's hand. God encourages an attitude of watchful patience as God condemns idolatry and assures Habakkuk of the Lord's constancy and the ultimate importance of faith. The rays emitting from the hand of God in this picture allude to God's power as described in Habakkuk 3:4.

Although Habakkuk does not receive an explicit answer to his questions about evil, what he receives is apparently enough. The book of Habakkuk closes with exultation and rejoicing as Habakkuk recognizes God as his strength, the source of his salvation, and the guiding presence in his life. (Habakkuk 1-3)

For my people have committed two evils: they have forsaken me, the fountain of living water, and dug out cisterns for themselves, cracked cisterns that can hold no water.
Jeremiah 2:13

Jeremiah, known as the weeping prophet, kneels among the signs of the peoples' abandonment of God and his way. The book of Jeremiah spans more than sixty years of Jewish history. At the time Jeremiah begins to write, the people of Israel have forsaken God and lost the Book of the Law.

In the illustration Jeremiah kneels before a fountain of water. God is the fountain of living water, and God decries the people for having abandoned the true God for false gods. God equates those false gods to man-made cisterns, broken and unable to hold water. The people worship gods that are in fact no gods at all. The image of a broken cistern leaking water stands in the foreground.

King Josiah instigates a renovation of the Temple five years after Jeremiah begins his prophecies about Israel's condition as an apostate nation. During the renovation the Book of the Law is found. Josiah attempts to return the people to God and meets with mixed success. After Josiah is killed in battle, his son briefly succeeds him on the throne. Within months, however, the Egyptian pharaoh imprisons the new king and places his own puppet king, Jehoiakim, on the throne of Judah. During this time, God denounces the people through Jeremiah for forsaking the Law and abandoning his ways. This condemnation is represented by the broken tablets of the Law seen on either side of the fountain of water. It is during this period that the prophet Habakkuk also records his oracles. (Jeremiah 2, 9)

I prophesied as he commanded me, and the breath came into them, and they lived, and stood on their feet, a vast multitude.
Ezekiel 37:10

Ezekiel, a priest in Jerusalem, becomes a prophet after Nebuchadnezzar exiles the Israelites to Babylon. God reveals to Ezekiel the future of Israel and, in obedience, Ezekiel proclaims God's revelations to his fellow captives.

Ezekiel speaks fervently and lives symbolically the prophecies that God gives him. Initially, Ezekiel preaches the coming destruction of the Temple to the exiles in the labor camps. Those prophecies combined with the exile and the accompanying slavery produce hopelessness among the Israelites.

However, once the prophecies come to pass and Jerusalem and the Temple are razed by the Babylonians under the leadership of Nebuchadnezzar, God begins to give Ezekiel visions of restoration. One of these visions is illustrated in the window. Ezekiel,

guided by the Spirit of God, first sees a valley of dry bones; the bones are many and very dry. They symbolize the entire house of Israel in their current state of despair. In the vision God causes the bones to rise and reassemble, then lays flesh and muscle on them. Finally, God calls on Ezekiel to summon the breath from the four winds to breathe into the whole, but lifeless, bodies. The bodies stand and live.

The prophecy of the dry bones is God's promise to raise the house of Israel, to bring the people back to their land, and to put God's spirit within them that they might know God as well as know God's words and actions. Indeed, the need for the house of Israel to understand that God is the sovereign Lord seems to be the primary purpose of Ezekiel's entire life of prophecy. (Ezekiel 37)

When [the king] came near the den where Daniel was, he cried out anxiously to Daniel, "O Daniel, servant of the living God, has your God whom you faithfully serve been able to deliver you from the lions?" Daniel 6:20

While Jeremiah and Ezekiel faithfully accomplish the ministries assigned to them during the Babylonian exile, God strategically places Daniel in the palace of Nebuchadnezzar. Daniel, an intelligent, noble youth of the tribe of Judah, resolves that he will not defile himself while in Babylon.

The Babylonians honor Daniel and the God he serves after witnessing a series of events that take place under numerous kings. Daniel demonstrates wisdom and intellect, interprets Nebuchadnezzar's dreams, foretells the fall and division of the Babylonian kingdom, and distinguishes himself as a man of excellent spirit. Daniel is eventually promoted to a prominent level within the kingdom. When King Darius decides to choose Daniel as his grand vizier, jealousy arises among the other presidents and the satraps. They conspire against Daniel and devise a scheme that takes advantage of Daniel's devotion to God.

The resulting edict prohibits praying to anyone but King Darius himself. Although Daniel knows that the decree has been passed and that the penalty of prayer to God is being thrown to the lions, he continues faithfully to pray in his usual way. Though the king regrets his decree, Daniel is nevertheless thrown into the lions' den as required by the edict.

The scene in the tracery depicts Daniel, portrayed with a blue halo and surrounded by sitting lions, looking toward the king, who is calling out to discover whether Daniel's God has indeed saved him. (Daniel 6)

Take courage, all you people of the land, says the Lord; work, for I am with you, says the Lord of hosts, according to the promise that I made you when you came out of Egypt. My spirit abides among you; do not fear.
Haggai 2:4b-5

After seventy years in exile the Jews are allowed to return to Jerusalem by the decree of King Cyrus. They immediately begin building the temple. Soon, however, a variety of obstacles cause the work on the project to stop. Fifteen years go by before the prophet Haggai receives a mandate from God to proclaim the need for immediately completing the temple. Haggai implores the governor, the high priest, and all the people still in Jerusalem to consider their priorities. They have taken the time to build homes of paneled wood, a luxury, yet have ignored God's house. Along with the challenge to examine their priorities, Haggai encourages them to be courageous and dauntless in their attempts to finish the temple. After work resumes, Haggai continues to proclaim the Lord's encouragement and assurances among the Jews living in Jerusalem. (Haggai 1-2)

Then I said, "What are these, my lord?" The angel who talked with me said to me, "I will show you what they are."
Zechariah 1:9

Zechariah, a contemporary of Haggai, also prophesies to the Israelites living in Jerusalem. The prophecies that Zechariah receives begin with a call to repentance. God implores the people to return to the Lord of hosts, that the Lord of hosts might return to them. Zechariah's subsequent prophecies bring hope and comfort to the people working to rebuild the temple.

In the vision depicted in the window, an angel of God stands speaking to Zechariah while in the background a rider sits on horseback among the myrtle trees. Although Scripture describes this vision as a rider on a red horse, with white, sorrel, and red horses behind him, our window depicts the scene with a rider in red, mounted on a white horse. The other horses, one of which is just visible behind the mounted rider, represent patrols of the earth, which have been sent out by the Lord. The angel speaking with Zechariah brings word of God's compassion, comfort, and restoration and directs Zechariah to proclaim this word to the people. (Zechariah 1)

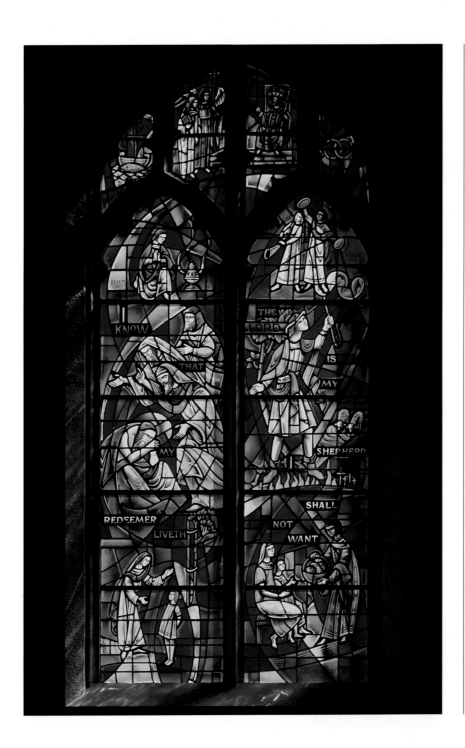

POETRY & WISDOM

... I know that my Redeemer liveth,
Job 19:25a
The Lord is my shepherd; I shall not want.
Psalm 23:1

Job, sitting in deepest anguish, dominates the left lancet. His three friends, Eliphaz, Bildad, and Zophar, stand over him attempting to counsel him in his severe grief. The friends' poor guidance, in the midst of Job's despair, causes Job additional misery. Yet Job rises up with the words of hope found in the left lancet: "I know that my Redeemer liveth." Directly opposite Job, in the right lancet, is an illustration of the twenty-third Psalm of David. The shepherd, staff in hand, stands firm as flames and thorns surround his feet. The sheep drinking from still waters are to the right.

The top of each lancet illustrates an additional Psalm; the left reflects a Psalm of repentance, and the right a Psalm of thanksgiving. Below Job is a representation of Proverbs 22:6, which speaks of raising children, and the bottom of the right lancet honors the virtuous woman of Proverbs 31. These four illustrations are the only ones in the sanctuary that include specific Scripture references.

The tracery, reading from right to left, depicts two gold rings symbolic of marriage and the Song of Solomon. The two center panels show what is frequently taken to be the implicit allegorical meaning of the Song of Solomon: the Bride of Christ being wed to Jesus, the King of kings. The left panel shows a boat, representing the church, with a remora attached below the water, representing Jesus Christ, like the celebrated fish, able to sustain the church in any storm.

"My spirit is broken, my days are extinct, the grave is ready for me. Surely there are mockers around me, and my eye dwells on their provocation."
Job 17:1

Job, a righteous man of God, loses all ten of his children and the entirety of his wealth in a single day. Following these catastrophes, Job loses his health. Here Job sits in darkest despair as his three friends, Eliphaz, Bildad, and Zophar, hover above him. The friends, who initially come and compassionately sit in silent empathy and mourning with him, vehemently speak out against Job. In their efforts to make sense of Job's excruciating suffering, Job's friends attempt to cast Job in the wrong. Instead of bringing comfort and solace to Job, they instead intensify Job's anguish. This attitude is symbolized by the pointing finger of the friend in the foreground and the way the friends seem to loom over the suffering Job. Yet, Job continues in conversation with both his friends and his God. As a result, at this most depressing of times, Job is able to rise up and proclaim the verse which is inlaid in the left lancet: "I know that my redeemer liveth!" (Job 1-42)

The Lord is my shepherd, I shall not want.
Psalm 23:1

This illustration of the twenty-third Psalm, a Psalm of David, shows the shepherd with his staff in hand, providing security and comfort to his sheep. The two sheep in the background drink from the still waters as

they pasture on the green fields. Both the thorns and fire at the feet of the shepherd allude to the valley of the shadow of death. Thorns, which can signify anguish, sin, and trials, seem fitting symbols of the valley, as do the flames , which can denote martyrdom. Barely visible to the right of the licking flames stands a row of bare white crosses. These too may symbolize the valley of death. However, the crosses might also be symbolic of the paths of righteousness in which the shepherd leads his flock and the restoration of the soul, which the Psalmist mentions. This reading of the cross symbolism adds a distinctly New Testament twist to the illustration, bringing to mind Jesus' words, "I am the good shepherd. The good shepherd lays down his life for the sheep." (John 10:11) This illustration gives rise to the verse found in the right lancet of this window: "The Lord is my shepherd, I shall not want." This verse blends particularly well with the Proverb immediately below the shepherd, the Proverb of the virtuous woman providing for the poor. (Psalm 23)

Create in me a clean heart, O God, and put a new and right spirit within me.
Psalm 51:10

This is a Psalm of David written after the prophet Nathan confronts King David regarding his adultery with Bathsheba and the subsequent murder of her husband Uriah. In this psalm David focuses on repentance and a plea for the restoration of his spirit according to the mercy and loving kindness of God. The censer holding incense that visibly wafts upward in the illustration is a symbol of prayer in use since the very beginning of church symbolism. This is a result of both an Old Testament reference (Psalm 141:2a) "Let my prayer be counted as incense before you," and a New Testament reference (Revelation 5:8b) "Each holding a harp and golden bowls full of incense, which are the prayers of the saints." (Psalm 51)

Make a joyful noise to the Lord, all the earth. Psalm 100:1

Psalm 100 is a song of thanksgiving, encouraging all to make a joyful noise, to worship with gladness, and to sing in God's presence. The trumpet often symbolizes a call to worship, and cymbals most frequently indicate loud and resounding praise. This attitude of jubilant, enthusiastic praise and worship reflects the mood of the hundredth Psalm. Psalm 100 also reminds us that we are the sheep of God's pasture, yet another Scriptural reminder of God as our shepherd. (Psalm 100)

Train children in the right way, and when old, they will not stray.
Proverbs 22:6

In this vignette a mother gestures as she instructs her child. The child listens intently. In the background, a young sapling tree tied to an upright

stake grows straight as it follows the path imposed upon it. Just as a stake provides for straight growth as the tree matures, so God's way provides training for the growth of children as they mature into adults. (Proverbs 22:6)

She opens her hand to the poor, and reaches out her hands to the needy. Proverbs 31:20

A woman and child receive a basket of food and provisions from the virtuous woman of Proverbs 31. This excellent wife, as some translations call her, exemplifies an attitude of thoughtful generosity. Showing the virtuous woman opening her hands to the poor demonstrates one way God fulfills the highlighted Scripture of the right lancet. Indeed, those who have the Lord as their shepherd shall not want, in part because his righteous ones provide necessities for the poor and needy. (Proverbs 31:10-31)

Look, O daughters of Zion, at King Solomon, at the crown with which his mother crowned him on the day of his wedding, on the day of the gladness of his heart. Song of Solomon 3:11

41

Two entwined, gold, circular bands represent the marriage in the Song of Solomon. Gold is symbolic of marriage, which is supposed to be indissoluble by anything but death. Likewise, gold is supposedly indissoluble by anything other than Aqua Regia, a yellowish chemical used primarily for dissolving gold and platinum.

The Song of Solomon, a poetic book about passion, love and marriage, is unquestionably a love song, the word *love* appearing more than thirty times in the eight short chapters of this book. Traditionally sung at the Jewish Passover, the people of Israel understood the Song of Solomon to be an allegory of God's love for his chosen people. As early as the second century after Christ, Christian writers began to see the Song of Solomon as an allegory of the love of God. They specifically held that the Song of Solomon is properly understood as an allegory of the marriage between Jesus Christ and the church. (Song of Solomon 1-8)

"Let us rejoice and exult and give him the glory, for the marriage of the Lamb has come, and his bride has made herself ready; to her it has been granted to be clothed with fine linen, bright and pure" – for the fine linen is the righteous deeds of the saints.
Revelation 19:7-8

An angel stands presenting the bride to Christ. The cross-topped staff in the angel's hand symbolizes the angel's heavenly position and authority. The bride is clothed in white, the color of purity, symbolic of the righteous deeds of the saints.

42

The bride holds a book in her right hand. The book symbolizes the role played by the word of God in bringing the church, and believers individually, to Christ. Jesus Christ sits crowned upon his throne. His crown is of gold, the color of Christ's kingly office, and he holds a scepter tipped by a barely visible cross. The scepter together with the crown and the tri-radiant nimbus on his head definitively mark the figure on the throne as Christ the King. (Revelation 19:1-10, 21:1-9)

And he has put all things under his feet and has made him the head over all things for the church, which is his body, the fullness of him who fills all in all.
Ephesians 1:22-23

The left pane of the tracery depicts a symbol of the church and the unfailing protection of Jesus Christ. The boat portrays the church and is a frequent symbol for the collective body of believers. The fish under the boat is a remora, a fish of ancient folklore that, though small, is supernatural in strength. The remora is supposedly able to attach itself to the keel of a boat and thereby prevent it from capsizing in any storm, no matter how mighty. The fish, along with the mast portrayed as a Chi Rho, the ancient monogram of Christ, represents Jesus Christ and the protection he is able to give to the church, regardless of the severity of the tribulations she encounters. (Matthew 16:18, Ephesians 1:22-23, 5:23; Colossians 1:18)

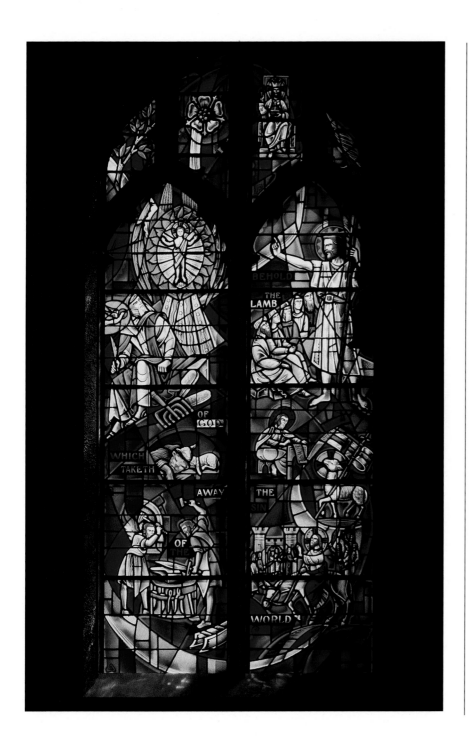

PREPARATION FOR THE MESSIAH

Behold the Lamb of God, which taketh away the sin of the world.
John 1:29b

This window is the last of the nave windows on the lectern side. It is in essence a culmination of a major underlying theme throughout all of the Old Testament windows - the preparation for the coming Messiah. Beginning with the Creation window, certain of the stories and prophecies have been thematically pointing to a coming Messianic victor.

This last Old Testament window focuses on the theme of preparation for the coming Messiah using two primary examples. The first example is the vision of Malachi, the last of the Old Testament prophets, in the left lancet. His oracle, given approximately four hundred years before Christ, depicts a coming Messiah that will bring healing and joy. Malachi's prophecies also reveal the mission of the prophet who will be the forerunner of the Christ, John the Baptist.

The second example is that of John the Baptist, shown in the right lancet. John prepares the way for Jesus to come by preaching repentance. John also identifies Jesus of Nazareth as the Lamb of God and proclaims Jesus' purpose, to take away the sin of the world. The verse in the window, taken directly from John's words to two of his disciples, emphasizes this. The other symbols within the window represent Jesus as the offspring of Jesse, the Messianic rose, and the victorious king.

43

But for you who revere my name the sun of righteousness shall rise, with healing in its wings.
Malachi 4:2a

Malachi, the last prophet of the Old Testament, sits surrounded by symbols of his oracle. The dove on Malachi's shoulder is symbolic of divine inspiration; the seven-branched candlestick represents Old Testament worship. Here, the candlestick lies overturned. The significance of this is found within the oracle of Malachi, for through Malachi's prophetic voice God reprimands Israel for profane worship that shows no honor or respect for God. Unworthy offerings, false pledges, and an attitude of disdain are three of the specifics for which God chastises the people. The overturned tablets represent God's condemnation of the temple priests because of the corruption of their teachings. God reproves the priests for their failure to instruct God's people and to walk themselves in God's ways, thereby leading God's people astray. The quill in Malachi's hand alludes to the book of remembrance, which includes all who revere and esteem the Lord.

Dominating this vignette of Malachi is a Messianic figure of the Christ — the sun of righteousness, risen with healing in its wings. A tri-radiant nimbus surrounds the Christ child's head, and a *vesica piscis* aureole encloses the entire figure of Christ. This same shape is apparent in both the Chancel window, framing the freestanding cross, and in the first of the prophet windows, where Jesus treads the wine press. Completing Malachi's prophecy, the wings of healing are evident on either side of the aureole, while rays of power alternate with flames of glory beneath it. The promise revealed to Malachi of coming righteousness, health, and joy precedes an injunction to remember the teachings of Moses, and a final promise that the prophet Elijah is to come before the day of the Lord. (Malachi 1-4)

They shall beat their swords into plowshares, and their spears into pruning hooks; nation shall not lift up sword against nation, neither shall they learn war any more.
Isaiah 2:4b-c

The prophets Isaiah and Micah, prophesying at approximately the same time in history, tell of the last days, when people of all nations will come to Jerusalem, eager to learn and live out the ways of God. Peace will be a sign of the kingdom. Weapons of war, swords and spears, will be transformed into tools of well-being, plowshares and pruning hooks. In this pictorial of the last days two men stand in front of a forger's furnace hammering a sword and spear. A finished plowshare lies positioned in the foreground while the flames of the forger's fire lick out the side of the oven. Interestingly, in the Hebrew text, the section of prophecy translated above is identical in both Isaiah and Micah. (Isaiah 2:1-4, Micah 4:1-5)

A shoot shall come out from the stump of Jesse, and a branch shall grow out of his roots.
Isaiah 11:1

Isaiah prophesies that a descendant of Jesse, King David's father, will have the spirit of the Lord and will demonstrate it by wisdom, understanding, counsel, might, knowledge, and fear of the Lord. He will be known by his righteousness and faithfulness, and through him peace will come to the land.

Both of the New Testament genealogies trace Jesus of Nazareth's lineage through Jesse. Additionally, in both Acts and Romans, Paul specifically refers to Jesus as a descendant of Jesse.

The branch as a Messianic symbol also derives from Old Testament prophecies that do not specifically mention Jesse. In Jeremiah God proclaims the raising up of a righteous branch with the branch's justice and righteousness highlighted. Then in Zechariah the name "the Branch" refers to God's servant, the Messiah, whom God will bring forth.
(Isaiah 11:1-10; Jeremiah 23:5, 33:15; Zechariah 3: 8, 6:12-13; Matthew 1:1-17; Luke 3:23-38; Acts 13:16-43; Romans 15:7-13)

The wolf shall live with the lamb, the leopard shall lie down with the kid, the calf and the lion and the fatling together, and a little child shall lead them.
Isaiah 11:6

Representing the peaceable kingdom promised by God, a lamb and a lion lie down together. As the meekest of animals, the lamb is a fitting image of helplessness in the face of the symbolically strongest of animals, the lion. This idea of a peaceable kingdom is found in both of the below referenced passages in Isaiah. Both sections mention animals dwelling peacefully together, although a lion and a lamb are never the pair depicted lying together. Rather, the wolf and the lamb, and the lion and the calf, peacefully dwell together in the verses. Some consider the symbolism of the lamb and lion to be indicative of Christianity (the lamb) and Judaism (the lion) peacefully co-existing.

Within the book of Hosea as well, God outlines an idea of safety from animals and from war. A previous vignette, that of swords being beaten into plowshares, reflects this. (Isaiah 11:6-9, 65:25; Hosea 2:16-20)

The wilderness, and the solitary place, shall be glad for them; and the desert shall rejoice, and blossom as the rose.
Isaiah 35:1 KJV

45

This stylistic form of the rose is a Rose of Sharon or Messianic Rose and is a symbol of the promised Messiah. In use only since the thirteenth century AD, it frequently occurs in Gothic architecture, both in stained glass windows and in woodcarvings.

The newer versions of the Bible translate the word *rose* in the Isaiah 35 passage as *crocus*. However, because of the King James Version translation and the Song of Solomon verse, this stylized antique rose traditionally symbolizes the promised Messiah.

Our sanctuary duplicates this same rose in ten woodcarvings on either side of the chancel window. Within the liturgical year this symbol is most frequently seen during Advent.
(Isaiah 35, Song of Solomon 2:1)

John said to the crowds that came out to be baptized by him, "You brood of vipers! Who warned you to flee from the wrath to come?"
Luke 3:7

John the Baptist stands speaking to a group that has gathered around him. As the last prophet before the Christ, John prepares the way for Jesus by preaching both repentance and the imminent coming of the Messiah. The staff John holds has half of a horizontal crossbar. This is symbolic that the crucifixion has not yet occurred. Perhaps John's pointing finger is illustrative of his preaching, which boldly calls the people to repentance. Or perhaps his upheld finger points out to his disciples that Jesus is the Lamb of God, the one who takes away the sin of the world, as John the Baptist proclaims in the gospel of John. The passage embedded in this window is that same proclamation that Jesus is the Lamb of God. (Isaiah 40:3, Malachi 3:1, Matthew 3:1-12, Mark 1:1-8, Luke 3:1-17, John 1:6-9, 19-28)

46

[Zechariah] asked for a writing tablet and wrote, "His name is John."
Luke 1:63a

The first of these two vignettes picture Zechariah, John the Baptist's father, writing the name of his son. This occurs on the day of John's circumcision and is necessary because of events surrounding the news of John's conception. Zechariah is offering incense in the temple, an honor assigned by lots and permitted a priest only once in a lifetime, when the angel Gabriel appears to him. Gabriel explains to Zechariah that God has heard his prayers for a child, and that Zechariah and Elizabeth will conceive. The child's name is to be John. Further, Gabriel proclaims that the Holy Spirit will fill John from birth and that John will carry out the mission of making the people ready for the coming Messiah. Zechariah expresses doubt about Gabriel's words, as he and his wife Elizabeth are both elderly. Because of Zechariah's doubt, Gabriel strikes him mute until all that Gabriel has foretold should come about.

On the day of John's circumcision, eight days after his birth as required by Jewish law, a question arises as to the baby's name. Zechariah, still unable to speak, writes for the gathered relatives that the name of the baby is to be John. It is with this act of obedience that Zechariah once again is able to speak and he launches into praise to God. (Luke 1:1-25, 57-80)

The second vignette is that of the nimbed Lamb of God holding the banner of victory. Although the Lamb is symbolic of Jesus Christ and his victory over sin and death at the cross, this same lamb when shown standing on a closed book is the most typical shield symbol used to represent John the Baptist, for his proclamation that Jesus is the Lamb of God. (John 1:29-36)

Lo, your king comes to you; triumphant and victorious is he, humble and riding on a donkey, on a colt, the foal of a donkey.
Zechariah 9:9b

On the left, Jesus sits crowned on his throne holding an orb topped by a cross, a symbol of his glorification and his triumph over the sin of the world. The Zechariah prophecy indicates Jesus will be triumphant and victorious. On the right is a palm frond, symbol of Jesus' triumphal entry into Jerusalem on the first Palm Sunday. Jesus enters Jerusalem on a donkey as prophesied. The crowd lays cloaks and branches on the road as they joyously shout, "Hosanna to the Son of David," proclaiming Jesus to be the King of Israel. (Zechariah 9:9, Matthew 21:8, Mark 11:8-10, John 12:12-19)

Jesus found a young donkey and sat on it; as it is written: "Do not be afraid, daughter of Zion. Look, your king is coming, sitting on a donkey's colt!"
John 12:14-15

Jesus rides into Jerusalem on a donkey. The people of Jerusalem, gathering for the celebration of the Passover, excitedly hail Jesus as the Son of David and the King of Israel. This sets in motion the coming sacrifice of Jesus at the hands of the authorities, as the Jewish leaders become increasingly disturbed at his popularity and power. (Matthew 21:1-11, Mark 11:1-10, Luke 19:28-40, John 12:9-19)

47

48

THE ANNUNCIATION

And she shall bring forth a son, and thou shalt call his name Jesus.
Matthew 1:21a

The three windows on the lectern side of the sanctuary light the upper stairwell leading to the balcony. Each window tells of a separate event happening before the birth of Jesus. The left window portrays the Annunciation, with the angel Gabriel standing over the Virgin Mary. The middle window shows Joseph dreaming of the child, Jesus. Both the angel and the dove indicate the divine nature of this baby that will be of the Holy Spirit. The final window shows Mary visiting her cousin Elizabeth who is noticeably pregnant with her own child, John the Baptist.

These windows, along with the corresponding gallery windows on the pulpit side, are the only windows in our sanctuary not designed by Marguerite Gaudin. Colum Sharkey designed the gallery windows, as well as those in the Chapel. There are subtle artistic differences between the two artists' work and a noticeable difference in the placement of the Scripture within the windows. The gallery window verses begin in the upper left and read down, but when the words reach the center window the Scripture reads up and to the right before sweeping down the third window.

And [Gabriel] came to her and said, "Greetings, favored one! The Lord is with you."
Luke 1:28

The angel Gabriel stands over the Virgin Mary with his right hand held in a position of benediction. He announces Mary's favor with God and the news that she will conceive a child that will be the Son of the Most High, an heir to the throne of David. Mary sits with her head bowed and hands held in a prayerful position, bringing to mind the humble acceptance Mary exhibits in her words, "Here am I, the servant of the Lord." Mary's cloak is blue, the color most frequently used for Mary. The flower springing up at her feet is a stylized lily. This flower appears in practically all renderings of the Annunciation. The lily itself symbolizes virginity and purity. (Luke 1:26-38)

But just when [Joseph] had resolved to do this, an angel of the Lord appeared to him in a dream and said, "Joseph, son of David, do not be afraid to take Mary as your wife, for the child conceived in her is from the Holy Spirit."
Matthew 1:20

When the righteous and merciful Joseph discovers that Mary is pregnant, he decides to quietly terminate the marriage arrangements. However, before Joseph can act, an angel of the Lord appears to him in a dream, bringing him the news that the child is of the Holy Spirit. The angel reveals that Joseph is to marry Mary as planned and name the child Jesus. The window presents the angel, feet in the air as if flying down from heaven, with hands around Joseph's head as the angel speaks the words of reassurance. The infant Jesus appears in the center of the pane with a dove flying near. The dove is symbolic of the part played by the Holy Spirit in the child's conception. (Matthew 1:18-25)

In those days Mary set out and went with haste to a Judean town in the hill country, where she entered the house of Zechariah and greeted Elizabeth.
Luke 1:39-40

49

Mary, walking staff in hand, arrives at her cousin's home. Elizabeth, previously barren and now advancing in years, is six months pregnant. The baby she carries is John the Baptist, the one promised to her husband Zechariah by the angel Gabriel. Elizabeth greets Mary with one hand outstretched in welcome, the other resting on her unborn child. As Mary greets Elizabeth the child in Elizabeth's womb leaps, occasioning the older woman's exclamation that blesses both Mary and her child. Mary's response is what we know as the *Magnificat*, mighty words of praise to God. (Luke 1:5-58)

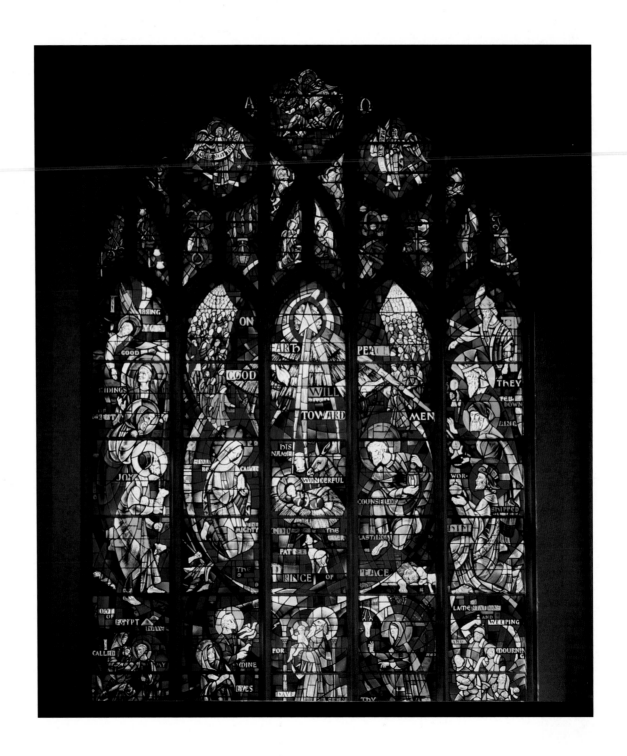

THE
CHRISTMAS WINDOW

…his name shall be called Wonderful, Counsellor,
The mighty God, The everlasting Father, The Prince
of Peace.
Isaiah 9:6b

… I bring you good tidings of great joy,
Luke 2:10b

… on earth peace, good will toward men.
Luke 2:14b

For mine eyes have seen thy salvation,
Luke 2:30

…they…fell down, and worshipped him:
Matthew 2:11b

…Out of Egypt have I called my son.
Matthew 2:15b

…lamentation(s), and weeping, and mourning,
Matthew 2:18b

The great façade window depicts, in both pictorial and Scriptural detail, the incarnation of Jesus Christ our Savior. The central figure of the window is the baby Jesus in the manger, emphasizing the crucial role of the Christ child in the world. The shepherds on the left and the wise men on the right flank the scene of the nativity. An angel directs the shepherds, while a devious King Herod points the wise men to Bethlehem. Underneath the manger scene the faithful Simeon, with Anna standing nearby, holds the baby Jesus during the presentation at the temple. In the top of the window angels instruct a dreaming Joseph. Warned in one of these dreams to flee with Mary and Jesus, Joseph obediently leads his family to Egypt, as shown in the bottom left panel. In the final scene, bottom right, soldiers slaughter the innocent babies of Bethlehem at Herod's command. The window also includes symbols for each of the original twelve disciples as well as symbols for each of the gospel writers.

And she gave birth to her firstborn son and wrapped him in bands of cloth, and laid him in a manger, because there was no place for them in the inn.
Luke 2:7

The birth of Jesus is the focal illustration of the great façade window. The baby Jesus lies wrapped in swaddling clothes in the manger, upon his head a cruciform nimbus. Mary kneels to the left of the manger as Joseph kneels on the opposite side and gazes into the face of Jesus. The candle in Joseph's hand serves as a reminder that Jesus is the Word, the light of the world, which has now entered creation as a baby. The ox and ass are frequently used together to symbolize the nativity. An ox, symbolic of sacrifice, and an ass, symbolic of humble service, both linger side by side behind the manger. The single lamb standing in front of the manger can be taken as representative of the believer. This is particularly appropriate when combined with the multitudes coming in from either side of the nativity scene. This Jesus will cause many to believe, and they will seek him out both individually and in great crowds.

The star above the manger shines brightly toward the Christ child as well as toward the wise men that are shown in the lancet to the right of Joseph. The five-pointed star of the Epiphany signifies the revealing of the Son of God to the world, but particularly to the Gentile nations.

On either side of this central, circular illustration are vignettes referring to Old Testament prophecies that speak of a coming time of peace. Outside the circle to the left is a hand holding swords that are being broken and turned into ploughshares. Outside the circle to the right are a lion and a lamb lying down together, symbolic of the peaceable kingdom. (Luke 2:1-7; Isaiah 2:4, 11:6-9, 65:25; Micah 4:3)

But the angel said to them, "Do not be afraid; for see – I am bringing you good news of great joy for all the people: to you is born this day in the city of David a Savior, who is the Messiah, the Lord."
Luke 2:10

To the left of the Nativity vignette, an angel hovers overhead announcing to the shepherds the birth of a Savior, the Messiah. A heavenly host joins the angel in praise to God. After the angels depart into heaven, the shepherds decide to go into Bethlehem to discover this amazing thing for themselves. Hastily they set out and find the infant Jesus with Mary and Joseph, just as the angel had described. The shepherds return to their field with joyous praise for God. (Luke 2:8-20)

Guided by the Spirit, Simeon came into the temple; and when the parents brought in the child Jesus, to do for him what was customary under the law, Simeon took him in his arms and praised God, ...
Luke 2:27-28a

The bottom center section of the window portrays Jesus' presentation in the temple. In the left panel Mary stands with her arms crossed gazing with wonder as Simeon holds the infant Jesus and prophesies. Joseph stands just behind Mary with their sacrificial offering of two turtledoves. Jesus and Simeon occupy the central position in this illustration. Simeon, a righteous and devout believer in God, gazes heavenward as he holds Jesus in his arms. Promised by the Holy Spirit that he would see the Christ before his death, Simeon blesses God, gives thanks, and proclaims the infant Jesus to be the Christ. Jesus faces outward with hand upraised in a symbol of benediction, crowned with a cruciform nimbus. Anna, the elderly widow and prophetess, occupies the panel on the right. As a woman of prayer and great devotion, she similarly praises God and proclaims Jesus to be the redemption of Israel. The lamp above Anna's hand possibly denotes Simeon's words to God in verse 32 that Jesus is a light bringing revelation to the Gentiles. (Luke 2:22-38)

53

When [the wise men] had heard the king, they set out; and there, ahead of them, went the star that they had seen at its rising, until it stopped over the place where the child was.
Matthew 2:9

Three wise men, representative of an unknown number of magi, occupy the bottom of this panel; at the top, a fourth figure, King Herod, sits on his throne pointing toward Bethlehem. The magi, or wise men, have come to Jerusalem from the Far East searching for the King of the Jews, whose star they have seen in the sky. Their desire is to worship him, and in anticipation of finding the infant king they hold gifts of gold, frankincense, and myrrh. The five-pointed star over the nativity scene is the star of the Epiphany, symbolic of the star that guides the magi to the place where the Christ child lives. The wise man in the forefront kneels, as a reminder that upon finding Jesus the wise men worship him with joy and present their gifts to him. In symbolic terms the gold refers to the kingly office of Jesus Christ, the Messiah. The frankincense, burned as a fragrant offering in worship, symbolically conveys the idea of deity. Finally, myrrh, an embalming spice, is a reference to Jesus' death.

Although King Herod insists that the wise men are to return to tell him of this king so that he too might go and worship him, he actually intends to destroy this possible threat to his kingdom. The magi are warned in a dream and they return to their country by a different route. (Matthew 2:1-12)

Now after they had left, an angel of the Lord appeared to Joseph in a dream and said, "Get up, take the child and his mother, and flee to Egypt, and remain there until I tell you; for Herod is about to search for the child, to destroy him."
Matthew 2:13

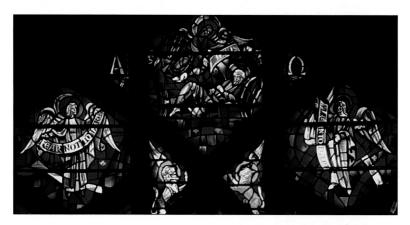

In the uppermost center panels of this window, a reclining Joseph sleeps. An angel holds over Joseph's head a banner that reads "Jesus," the name the angel proclaims to Joseph before Jesus is born. On either side of the sleeping Joseph are the Greek letters Alpha and Omega, yet another name for Jesus. This name for the Savior is found in the closing book of the New Testament, much as the name Jesus is first found in the opening book of the New Testament. Below the letters Alpha and Omega are two more angels, each

holding a banner. The two angels stand with wings and arms outstretched. The angel on the left holds a banner which reads, "Fear not to take," a reference to the first recorded appearance of an angel to Joseph when Joseph receives instructions he is to wed Mary as planned. The angel on the right holds a banner that reads, "flee into Egypt", a portion of the command God sends Joseph urging him to escape the coming destruction aimed at Jesus.
(Matthew 1:18-25, 2:13-14)

Then Joseph got up, took the child and his mother by night, and went to Egypt.
Matthew 2:14

Mary, conventionally clothed in blue, sits upon a donkey's back holding the baby Jesus as Joseph leads his small family away from Israel and into Egypt. Scripture stresses that this move into Egypt makes possible the fulfillment of an Old Testament prophecy found in Hosea 11:1. "Out of Egypt I called my son" is the portion of that verse expressed both within the Matthew passage and inscribed within this window panel. (Matthew 2:14-15, Hosea 11:1)

When Herod saw that he had been tricked by the wise men, he was infuriated, and he sent and killed all the children in and around Bethlehem who were two years old or under, according to the time that he had learned from the wise men.
Matthew 2:16

Once Herod realizes the wise men are not going to return to report their findings to him, he is enraged. In an attempt to destroy any possibility that the newly born king could be a threat to his rule, Herod orders the massacre of all the male children two years of age and younger in the vicinity of Bethlehem. Jesus escapes this slaughter of the innocents because of Joseph's obedience. This final vignette of the Christmas window, found in the right bottom-most corner, shows a horrific scene of Roman soldiers slaying babies and young children as their mothers attempt to shield them from the blows of death. Scripture points to this event as another fulfillment of an Old Testament prophecy, since the prophet Jeremiah foretells mothers weeping and mourning over their children. (Matthew 2:16-18, Jeremiah 31:15)

And when day came, he called his disciples and chose twelve of them, whom he also named apostles: Simon, whom he named Peter, and his brother Andrew, and James, and John, and Philip, and Bartholomew, and Matthew, and Thomas, and James son of Alphaeus, and Simon, who was called the Zealot, and Judas son of James, and Judas Iscariot, who became a traitor. Luke 6:13-16

In a band across the width of the Christmas window, symbols for each of the twelve apostles flank four central symbols that represent the four writers of the gospels, known as the Four Evangelists. Reading from left to right, the first symbol is a pair of crossed keys. This symbol corresponds to Simon, also called Peter. The meaning of the crossed keys is found in Matthew 16:19, when Jesus blesses Peter, declaring that Peter will be the foundation of the church, and that Jesus will give Peter the keys of heaven. These keys, crossed in the shape of an X, are the most typical symbol of Simon Peter. Additionally, a second symbol for Simon Peter is given in the same windowpane. The inverted cross signifies the crucifixion of Peter. Tradition holds that Peter, considering himself unworthy to be crucified in the same manner as his Lord, asked to be crucified head downward.

The second pane of this section represents James, the brother of John. Scriptural references to James include his presence at the Transfiguration, his inclusion among the three apostles taken aside by Jesus in the Garden of Gethsemane, and his witness of Jairus's daughter's healing. Because of his legendary pilgrimages, James is represented by symbols of pilgrimage. A pilgrim staff and wallet as well as three scallop shells witness to James's celebrated pilgrimages after the ascension of Jesus.

The last Scriptural reference to James is found in Acts 12:2, when King Herod orders James slain. The Acts of the Apostles window of our sanctuary depicts this event.

The pane above the symbols of pilgrimage symbolizes the Apostle John. John is known in Scripture as James's brother, a fisherman along with James and Peter. Like his brother James, Jesus includes John in witnessing the Transfiguration, the agony in the Garden of Gethsemane, and the raising of Jairus's daughter. Tradition holds that John is the author of both the gospel by his name and the book of the Revelation, as well as the writer of the three epistles of John. Given that there are so many scriptural references to the Apostle John, it is interesting that his symbol is taken from an event that is not found in the Bible. Legend holds that the Emperor Domitian made two attempts on John's life. In one, the Emperor orders John to drink poisoned wine, but before John can do so the poison disappears in the form of a snake slithering from the cup. Hence a symbol for John is a chalice from which a snake is rising, the symbol used in the window.

The fourth symbol is of two fish, crossed to form a St. Andrew's cross (in the shape of an X), and a boat hook. These symbols represent the Apostle Andrew. One of Jesus' earliest disciples, as well as Simon Peter's brother, it is Andrew who Scripture says first brought Simon Peter to Jesus. Both symbols, the great boat hook and the fish, represent Andrew's original occupation as a fisherman, as well as his renown as a great fisher of men. Indeed his evangelistic efforts were so prominent that it led to his death at the hands of a Roman governor in Greece. Supposedly,

the cross on which he was crucified was shaped like an X, hence the crossing of the fish.

Left of the symbols of the Four Evangelists is a pane that contains the symbols for two different apostles. In the top of the opening, three knives denote Bartholomew, believed to be Nathanael in the gospel of John. Tradition holds that Bartholomew was flayed alive by heathens as he returned from a missionary endeavor. Therefore, one of his more frequent symbols is of three knives, representing the means of his martyrdom. Below the knives is a basket out of which rises a Tau (T-shaped) cross. This is the symbol for the Apostle Philip. The basket refers to John 6, which tells of the feeding of the five thousand, where Jesus tested Philip by asking him how all the people were to be fed. Apparently the Tau cross refers to a legend that Philip was aided in eliminating serpent worship in one of the cities of Scythia by a cross.

The four center symbols are representative of the Four Evangelists: Matthew, Mark, Luke, and John. Each of the gospel writers corresponds to a particular winged creature. The fact that there are four of these winged beings is derived from both Ezekiel 1 and Revelation 4, where four living creatures surround the throne of God. Although throughout the centuries the identification of which creature is associated with which particular gospel writer has changed somewhat, the most current thinking and that ascribed to in our windows is as follows: the winged man in the lower center panel represents Matthew. The winged man depicts the gospel of Matthew because Matthew's gospel traces the human descent of Jesus, emphasizing Jesus' position as the legitimate heir of David. The winged lion symbolizes the Evangelist Mark. Mark opens with John the Baptist crying out in the desert, euphemistically roaring as a lion. The ox in the upper right center pane is representative of Luke. The ox, as a symbol of sacrifice, corresponds to the gospel of Luke, which includes a detailed account of the sacrificial death of Jesus. The winged eagle characterizes the gospel writer John, already symbolized in his role as disciple by the chalice and serpent. An eagle connotes John the evangelist because of the contemplations and writings of John. Whether it is F.R. Webber stating, "from first to last his Gospel soars on eagles' wings to the very throne of Heaven"[1] or George Ferguson asserting, "St. John, in his Gospel, soared upward in his contemplation of the divine nature of the Saviour,"[2] the soaring eagle has been understood as a fine match for the lofty ideas expressed by John.

Right of the Four Evangelists are symbols for the remaining six disciples. The first pane depicts both Thomas and James the Less. Three stones and a girdle represent Thomas. The stones indicate stoning, the first of the tortures he supposedly endured before being run through by a spear wielded by a pagan priest. The girdle as a symbol for Thomas springs from a legend that the Virgin Mary lowered her girdle from heaven to overcome Thomas's doubts.

The saw and fuller's bat are frequently used symbols for James, son of Alphaeus, also known as James the Less. They signify the means of his body's destruction. An ancient historian records that after having survived an attempt on his life, his pleas for forgiveness for his Jewish enemies so angered them that they stoned him, crushed his head with a fuller's bat, and then sawed his body asunder.

In the next panel three purses symbolize Matthew, identifying his occupation as a tax collector before Jesus called him. The battle-ax centered in the pane reflects Matthew's death by beheading.

A sailboat represents Jude, also called Judas son of James in the Luke passage, and believed to possibly be a brother of James the Less. Little is known about this apostle, but many believe he traveled with Simon the Zealot, spreading the gospel before being martyred for his witness in Persia. The sailboat represents his missionary endeavors.

The fish impaled upon a fishhook is the symbol for Simon the Zealot, also known as Simon the Canaanite. Little is known of Simon other than the tradition that says he evangelized extensively before his martyrdom. One interesting legend maintains that Simon was one of the shepherds in the field who beheld the angels announcing the birth of the Christ child.

The final disciple symbol is that of Judas Iscariot, the betrayer. Thirty pieces of silver curve across the bottom of the final pane, indicating the amount of money Judas was paid for betraying his innocent friend Jesus. Both the noose, hanging from the inverted L shape, and the letter J above it, created by what appears to be rope, represent Judas and his suicide by hanging.

(Matthew 10:2-4, Mark 3:16-19, Luke 6:12-19, Acts 1:13)

---

[1] FR Webber, Church Symbolism (Detroit: Omnigraphics, 1992) 188.

[2] George Ferguson, Signs & Symbols in Christian Art (London: Oxford University Press, 1961) 17.

THE CHILDHOOD OF JESUS

And the child grew, and waxed strong in spirit, filled with wisdom; and the grace of God was upon him.
Luke 2:40

In the first panel of these gallery windows Jesus is at home. Mary sits with her distaff as her husband, the carpenter Joseph, works alongside her. Jesus sits on the floor wielding the tools of his father's trade, the three-rayed nimbus clearly marking him as not merely human but also divine. The center panel illustrates Jesus at the age of twelve. In the temple, surrounded by the teachers of the Law, Jesus amazes them with both his questions and answers. The final section shows Jesus obediently returning home to Nazareth from Jerusalem with Mary and Joseph.

59

The child grew and became strong, filled with wisdom; and the favor of God was upon him.
Luke 2:40

As Joseph works with a saw, the boy Jesus sits wielding the tools of his father's carpentry trade. Mary sits nearby with a distaff, a hand tool for spinning, and looks toward Jesus. Even during the most mundane of human activity, the tri-radiant nimbus of gold and blue sets Jesus apart. It identifies Jesus as one of the Godhead. The entire vignette reminds us of both Jesus' humanity and his divinity. (Matthew 13:55; Mark 6:3; Luke 2:39-40, 51-52)

After three days they found him in the temple, sitting among the teachers, listening to them and asking them questions. And all who heard him were amazed at this understanding and his answers.
Luke 2:46-47

Within the walls of the Temple, the teachers of the Law surround the twelve-year-old boy Jesus. Jesus is speaking. His understanding of religious matters apparently astounds these experts in Jewish law, and the picture clearly shows the teachers both listening to Jesus and talking among themselves. This event occurs during an annual trip that Jesus and his parents take to Jerusalem for the Passover festival. Believing him to be with the crowd of friends and relatives traveling together back home, it takes Mary and Joseph three anxiety-filled days to finally find Jesus back in Jerusalem at the temple. His response is that he was in his Father's house where he belonged. (Luke 2:41-51)

Then he went down with them and came to Nazareth, and was obedient to them. His mother treasured all these things in her heart.
Luke 2:51

Jesus returns with Mary and Joseph from Jerusalem to their home in Nazareth. As they ascend the steps it seems Jesus reaches back to Mary, perhaps to explain why it was necessary for him to be in his Father's house. Both Mary and Joseph have questioning looks, and Scripture says they did not understand. Mary, just as she did with the words of the shepherds twelve years earlier, ponders the knowledge of these events in her heart.

Two additional symbols finish out this final panel of the childhood of Jesus. The first is a star of David, symbolic of Jesus' place as the offspring of David, the divinely appointed heir to King David's throne, yet coming through the human line of David. The second symbol is of the flame, or light, that hangs at the top of the steps. This symbol alludes to God's appearance to mankind in the person of Jesus, the Messiah. The symbol points us to Jesus as the Light of the world, the Son of God, both fully human and fully divine. (Luke 2:48-51)

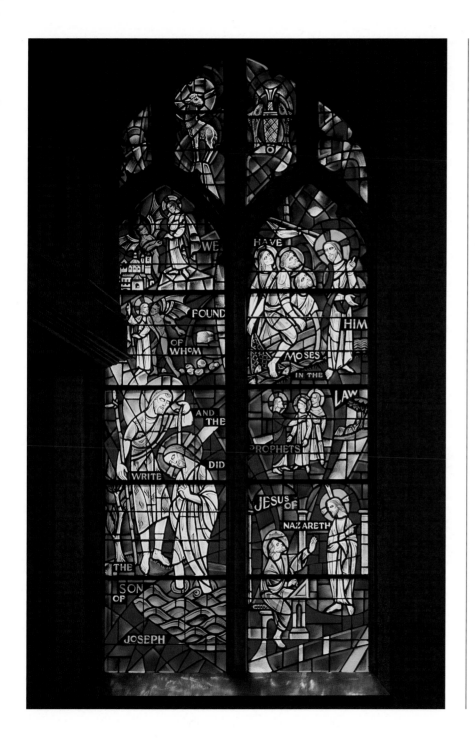

DISCIPLESHIP

We have found him, of whom Moses in the law, and the prophets, did write, Jesus of Nazareth, the son of Joseph. John 1:45b

This window contains three major discipleship themes: baptism, temptation, and the making of disciples. Beginning in the bottom left lancet, John baptizes Jesus in the Jordan.

Immediately following the baptism, the Spirit leads Jesus into the desert where Jesus fasts for forty days and is tempted by the devil. The top of the left lancet illustrates two of the three recorded temptations.

The Lamb of God in the tracery symbolizes John's metaphor for Jesus. Jesus is the Lamb of God that takes away the sin of the world, John tells his disciples.

The right lancet of the window depicts the calling of five of the twelve disciples. At the top of the lancet, Jesus calls Peter, James, and John to follow him. In the center, Jesus speaks to Nathanael as Philip watches. It is to the guileless Nathanael that Philip proclaims the words recorded in the window. The bottom of the right lancet shows Jesus calling to Matthew, the tax collector, as he sits at his booth.

The tracery yields one last symbol, that of a basket and fish. This ancient symbol of discipleship is reminiscent of Jesus' promise that he would make Peter, James, and John fishers of men.

61

Then Jesus came from Galilee to John at the Jordan, to be baptized by him.
Matthew 3:13

Jesus stands in the Jordan River as his cousin John baptizes him. The single crossbar on John's staff indicates that the crucifixion has yet to occur.

John objects to baptizing Jesus, declaring that he is not worthy to baptize such a one as he. Jesus persists, saying it is fitting for them in order to fulfill all righteousness. Although John balks at baptizing Jesus, he does not yet know that Jesus is the promised Messiah, the one for whom he is preparing a way. Jesus' posture of prayer is a reminder that it is while he is praying that heaven opens, the Spirit descends, and God's voice proclaims, "This is my Son, the Beloved, with whom I am well pleased." (Matthew 3:17) After this pronouncement from heaven the Spirit directs Jesus into the desert for forty days and nights.
(Matthew 3:13-17, Mark 1:9-11, Luke 3:21-22, John 1:29-34)

The tempter came and said to him, "If you are the Son of God, command these stones to become loaves of bread." But he answered, "It is written, 'One does not live by bread alone, but by every word that comes from the mouth of God.' "
Matthew 4:3-4

At the end of forty days of fasting in the desert the devil comes to Jesus, in order to tempt him. The first recorded temptation lures Jesus to prove he is the Son of God by turning some of the desert stones into bread to satisfy his hunger. In response Jesus quotes from the Law of Moses, pointing out that life comes from the word of God. In the illustration Jesus stands pointing to God in heaven, the source of life, as the tempter, depicted in purple and green, entices Jesus to turn the stones at which he is pointing into loaves of bread. (Matthew 4:1-4, Mark 1:12-13, Luke 4:1-4, Deuteronomy 8:3)

Again, the devil took him to a very high mountain and showed him all the kingdoms of the world and their splendor; and he said to him, "All these I will give you, if you will fall down and worship me."
Matthew 4:8-9

In another of the three recorded temptations, Jesus stands on a high mountain with the kingdoms of the world spread before him. The devil, showing Jesus an incredible array of earthly splendor and glory, offers to give it all to Jesus if he will humble himself and worship Satan. Jesus resists the temptation using God's command, as given to Moses, that it is God alone who is to be worshiped and served. (Matthew 4:8-11, Luke 4:5-8, Deuteronomy 6:13)

The next day he saw Jesus coming toward him and declared, "Here is the Lamb of God who takes away the sin of the world!"
John 1:29

The *Agnus Dei*, the Lamb of God, is one of the oldest Christian symbols. Always crowned by a three-rayed nimbus to signify divinity, it is included in this window to convey the identity of Jesus. John tells his disciples that Jesus is the Lamb of God shortly after Jesus' forty days in the wilderness.

John, who was to prepare a people for the Messiah, points out Jesus and explains that he is the Lamb of God. Two of John the Baptist's disciples, Andrew and presumably John (the Apostle), follow Jesus and spend the day with him. Their conversation with him convinces Andrew that Jesus is the Messiah and he brings Simon Peter, his brother, to meet Jesus. It is from these events that Jesus begins to form his band of disciples. (John 1:24-42)

Nathanael asked him, "Where did you get to know me?" Jesus answered, "I saw you under the fig tree before Philip called you."
John 1:48

In this illustration of Philip bringing Nathanael to Jesus there is a background depiction of someone asleep under a tree. Philip, called by Jesus to follow him, is convinced that Jesus is the Messiah. Eagerly Philip seeks out his friend Nathanael, shown here sleeping under a fig tree. Philip asserts that they have found the one written of by Moses, in the law and the prophets, and that the long awaited Messiah is none other than Jesus of Nazareth, the son of Joseph. It is Philip's statement from John 1:45 that is inscribed in the window. Nathanael, in keeping with his skeptical and honest personality, bluntly responds with doubt that any good thing could come out of Nazareth. Yet, when Nathanael meets Jesus, it takes only one brief exchange, revealing that Jesus has supernaturally seen Nathanael under the fig tree, for Nathanael to proclaim with conviction that Jesus is both the Son of God and the King of Israel. (John 1:43-51)

Then Jesus said to Simon, "Do not be afraid; from now on you will be catching people." When they had brought their boats to shore, they left everything and followed him.
Luke 5:10b-11

After Peter spends a long and unproductive night fishing, Jesus asks Peter to take him out on the lake of Gennesaret in order for him to teach the multitudes on the shore. Afterwards, Jesus instructs Peter to take the boat out into deep water and put out the nets once more. Though doubtful, Peter does as Jesus instructs. The nets fill with an incredible catch of fish; so large in fact that the nets begin to break and help must be called from a partnering boat manned by James and John, the sons of Zebedee. Once back on shore Peter, James, and John leave everything behind and follow Jesus.

These three will become Jesus' closest disciples. They will witness at least one healing not seen by the other disciples, the Transfiguration, and Jesus' agony in the Garden of Gethsemane. (Luke 5:1-11, with similar renditions in Matthew 4:18-22, Mark 1:16-20)

As Jesus was walking along, he saw a man called Matthew sitting at the tax booth; and he said to him, "Follow me." And he got up and followed him.
Matthew 9:9

In Capernaum Jesus teaches many people, and spectacularly heals a paralytic. This causes consternation and fury in some of the Jewish scribes, but causes awe and reverence for God among the crowds of people. It is after this healing that Jesus passes by Matthew's tax collection booth. Gazing intently at Matthew Jesus calls to him, "Follow me!" Matthew's response, like the reaction of Peter, James, and John, is to leave everything and immediately follow Jesus.

That evening Matthew gives a large banquet for Jesus, inviting tax collectors and others looked down upon by the scribes and Pharisees. The ridicule this sets off among the scribes and Pharisees causes Jesus to pronounce his reason for coming, to call sinners to repentance. (Matthew 9:9-13, Mark 2:13-17, Luke 5:27-32)

And he said to them, "Follow me, and I will make you fish for people."
Matthew 4:19

This symbol of a basket and three fish, two on either side and one in the basket, is a symbol of discipleship. The symbol derives from an ancient ring stone, worn by the German Bishop Arnold of Metz (582-641 AD). Discipleship is intricately tied to evangelism, or being a fisher of people. Bringing the good news of the gospel to people everywhere is a critical part of discipleship both because it is what Jesus himself did and taught his closest disciples to do, and because just before Jesus ascended into heaven he commanded his disciples to go and make disciples of all nations. (Matthew 4:18-19, 28:18-20; Mark 1:17; Luke 5:10)

JESUS TEACHING

For the Son of man is come to seek and to save that which was lost.
Luke 19:10

The verse of Scripture in this window sets the tone for what Jesus will teach and to whom Jesus will teach it. Starting in the bottom left lancet Jesus seeks to save Nicodemus, a ruling Pharisee. Above Nicodemus is the woman at the well. Totally unlike the moral and Jewish Nicodemus, the Samaritan woman is both living an immoral life with a man not her husband and worshiping in a way contrary to Jewish Law. However, Jesus seeks her out. In the top of the left lancet are the children whom Jesus welcomes with open arms. In the top of the right lancet Jesus comes to seek and save the distracted Martha and the devoted Mary. Below them, is the rich young ruler whom Jesus loves. In the bottom of the right lancet Zacchaeus perches in a sycamore tree as Jesus calls out to him.

Finally, shown in the tracery is the poor widow, so generously contributing out of her poverty. On either side of the tracery, the symbols of faith, hope, and love crown this window. And indeed, Jesus' teachings could well be summarized by these three words. Jesus taught about faith in God and in himself, God's Son. Jesus taught about hope in the coming kingdom of God. Finally Jesus taught about love, our need to love God above all else and God's overwhelming love for us. This love caused the Father to send his only Son to die on a cross in order to deliver us from death and give us eternal life.

65

Now there was a Pharisee named Nicodemus, a leader of the Jews. He came to Jesus by night and said to him, "Rabbi, we know that you are a teacher who has come from God; for no one can do these signs that you do apart from the presence of God."
John 3:1-2

Nicodemus, a Pharisee and member of the ruling Sanhedrin, as well as a teacher, comes to Jesus under the cover of darkness. The small crescent moon, just visible between Jesus' halo and hand, indicates nighttime. Perhaps the visit is in the evening because Jesus is already beginning to cause unease among the Jewish leaders. But Jesus' signs and teachings are intriguing enough to Nicodemus that he seeks Jesus out for himself. In this scene, Nicodemus sits at Jesus' feet in a posture of studious attention. In fact, Nicodemus's opening comment to Jesus emphasizes Jesus' role as a teacher. Jesus focuses the conversation on God, the Spirit, and himself, the Son of Man and also the Son of God.

Jesus' discussion with Nicodemus includes some of Christianity's most memorable verses. Jesus tells Nicodemus that one must be born anew to see the kingdom of God. Jesus also indicates that he will "be lifted up" (John 3:14) as Moses lifted the serpent in the wilderness, a reference to Jesus' eventual crucifixion. The symbol of a snake on a staff appears twice in our windows, in the tracery of the Moses window and in the tracery of the Jesus Healing window. Finally, in these verses is what Martin Luther called the gospel in miniature: "For God so loved the world, that he gave his only begotten Son, that whosoever should believeth in him should not perish, but have everlasting life." (John 3:16 KJV)
(John 3:1-21)

A Samaritan woman came to draw water, and Jesus said to her, "Give me a drink."
John 4:7

Leaving Judea and going back to Galilee, Jesus chooses to go through Samaria. On reaching the Samaritan city of Sychar, Jesus stops and sits by a well while his disciples go on to buy food. When a Samaritan woman approaches the well Jesus speaks to her, asking her for a drink. In the window the Samaritan woman holds her water jug. Jesus sits by the well, gesturing as he asks her for water.

Their conversation almost immediately takes on a spiritual dimension when Jesus proclaims that he can give living water that surges up to eternal life. As she questions Jesus further, he reveals that he knows about her many husbands and that the man she lives with now is not her husband. The woman declares Jesus a prophet, and as they talk further Jesus reveals to her that he is the Messiah.

After the disciples return, the woman leaves for the village and soon returns to the well with many of the townspeople, bringing them out to meet Jesus. They ask Jesus to stay with them and he does, for two days. Consequently many believe in Jesus, proclaiming him the Savior of the world. (John 4:1-42)

But the Lord answered her, "Martha, Martha, you are worried and distracted by many things; there is need of only one thing. Mary has chosen the better part, which will not be taken away from her."
Luke 10:41-42

As Jesus travels about Judea continuing his ministry Martha welcomes him into her home. In the pictorial Martha stands holding a bowl of fruit, keys around her waist, a broom behind her. The keys and broom are typical symbols of Martha. Mary, Martha's sister, kneels with hands folded, in a posture of devotion near Jesus' feet.

Martha busies herself with preparations in order to serve Jesus while Mary sits with Jesus. The busy and distracted Martha becomes angry that Mary is not helping serve. Mary chooses instead to sit and listen to Jesus speak. Martha is bold enough to take her complaint directly to Jesus, demanding that he tell Mary to help her. Jesus instead takes the opportunity to gently teach Martha that Mary has actually made the better choice. (Luke 10:38-42)

And he took them up in his arms, laid his hands on them, and blessed them.
Mark 10:16

All three synoptic gospels relate the story of Jesus blessing the children. In the window vignette Jesus sits with numerous children gathered around him. One sits on his lap and another kneels beside him, while

Jesus' arms seem to welcome and draw them closer. Two adults stand behind Jesus; they represent those bringing their children to Jesus that he might touch them and pray. The disciples try to turn the children away, feeling Jesus has more important work to do. But Jesus welcomes the children, using them as an example for his disciples.
(Matthew 19:13-15, Mark 10:13-16, Luke 18:15-17)

When the young man heard this word, he went away grieving, for he had many possessions.
Matthew 19:22

67

A wealthy young ruler eagerly approaches Jesus to seek the means of eternal life. As Jesus engages him in conversation the young man reveals that he has kept the commandments regarding his relationships with others. However, when Jesus instructs him to sell his many belongings and to follow him, the young ruler sadly turns away, apparently choosing his great wealth over Jesus. Jesus' hand, reaching out to the young man's shoulder as he dejectedly turns away, serves as a reminder that Jesus loves the young man and must be saddened himself at his refusal to follow.
(Matthew 19:16-30, Mark 10:17-31, Luke 18:18-30)

When Jesus came to the place, he looked up and said to him, "Zacchaeus, hurry and come down; for I must stay at your house today."
Luke 19:5

As Jesus passes through Jericho, he stops beneath a sycamore tree and calls Zacchaeus down. As the chief tax collector, Zacchaeus is both rich and despised. Because Zacchaeus is very short he is unable to see through the crowd so he climbs a tree. Zacchaeus's encounter with Jesus radically changes him. He volunteers half of all his belongings to the poor and offers to reimburse, fourfold, anyone he has defrauded. It is at this point that Jesus utters the verse shown in this window that "the Son of Man is come to seek and to save that which was lost." (Luke 19:1-10)

Then he called his disciples and said to them, "Truly I tell you, this poor widow has put in more than all those who are contributing to the treasury."
Mark 12:43

On seeing a poor widow generously give all she has, Jesus calls his disciples to him. He deliberately points out to his disciples, two of whom are shown standing behind Jesus, that she has given more than all of the wealthy people who have been contributing out of their abundance. In the tracery

depiction of this scene, the widow holds an infant in one arm as she places her offering into the treasury box.
(Mark 12:41-44, Luke 21:1-4)

And now faith, hope, and love abide, these three; and the greatest of these is love.
I Corinthians 13:13

Framing the previous vignette in the tracery are the three symbols: faith, hope, and love. The anchor is a widely used and accepted symbol of hope — "We have this hope, a sure and steadfast anchor of the soul." (Hebrews 6:19)

The cross, here depicted in one of its simplest forms, is symbolic of faith. Finally, the heart shown in the far right is symbolic of love. (Hebrews 6:19, Hebrews 12:2, I John 4:16)

68

JESUS PREACHING

Watch, and pray, that ye enter not into temptation; the spirit…is willing, but the flesh is weak.
Matthew 26:41

The illustrations within this window primarily represent Jesus' preaching and his public ministry. Dominating the left lancet is Jesus preaching what we call the Sermon on the Mount. Many disciples, not just the twelve, gather around to hear his authoritative discourse. Sharing the left lancet are two examples of parables, one of Jesus' primary means of preaching and teaching. At the top is the Good Samaritan and at the bottom is the parable of the Prodigal Son, complete with the younger son in the father's embrace, while the elder son still works in the field. The right lancet illustrates two more parables. At the bottom is the parable of the rich fool and just above is the parable of the Pharisee and the publican. The top of the right lancet depicts Jesus teaching his closest disciples to pray.

The tracery leaps ahead of the chronology of the windows and portrays Jesus' agony in the Garden of Gethsemane. An angel, holding a golden chalice, strengthens Jesus, as his three closest disciples sleep to the right, and a crowd of soldiers and Jews led by Judas approach to the left. The verse of Scripture in the window comes from Jesus' words to his disciples, after he finds them unable to remain awake while he prays in the garden. Although the primary focus of this window is Jesus' preaching, a secondary theme is prayer.

69

When Jesus saw the crowds, he went up the mountain; and after he sat down, his disciples came to him.
Matthew 5:1

Jesus' delivery of the Sermon on the Mount dominates this window. Jesus sits with arms raised on a stylized mountain with multitudes of disciples gathered around him. All the faces show rapt attention, portraying their amazement at the authority of Jesus' teaching.

Jesus begins his preaching with the Beatitudes and continues with the familiar analogies of his disciples' being the salt of the earth and the light of the world. (Matthew 5:1-7:29)

"But a Samaritan while traveling came near him; and when he saw him, he was moved with pity."
Luke 10:33

As Jesus teaches the people, he uses numerous parables to demonstrate his teaching, such as this one of the Good Samaritan. Robbers beat and rob a man before leaving him for dead on the side of the road. First a priest and then a Levite pass by the man without helping. But a Samaritan, apparently simply journeying through, takes time to help the man. Jews scorned Samaritans, a mixed race of people who worshiped God, but not in Jerusalem nor completely in keeping with Jewish law. In the window the Samaritan gives aid to the victim as the priest and the Levite, who chose not to help, pass by on the other side of the road. Jesus uses this parable to demonstrate whom we should consider our neighbors as well as to exemplify compassion. (Luke 10:25-37)

He was praying in a certain place, and after he had finished, one of his disciples said to him, "Lord, teach us to pray, as John taught his disciples."
Luke 11:1

Scripture holds two very similar versions of what we call the Lord's Prayer. Matthew records the first occurrence during the Sermon on the Mount, and Luke records the second. In the Luke account, portrayed here, one of the twelve disciples asks Jesus to teach them to pray as John had taught his disciples. Jesus stands before them with hands folded and head bowed in a posture of humble prayer. In addition to the succinct prayer found in Luke, Jesus encourages the disciples' persistence in prayer by adding a parable about two friends. During this discourse Jesus also assures the disciples that the Heavenly Father is available to give the Holy Spirit to everyone who asks. (Matthew 6:5-15, Luke 11:1-13)

"But God said to him, 'You fool! This very night your life is being demanded of you. And the things you have prepared, whose will they be?'"
Luke 12:20

As Jesus speaks to a large crowd, someone asks Jesus to arbitrate the distribution of a family inheritance. In reply, Jesus tells a parable pointing out the folly of relying solely on earthly treasure. The window illustration shows the rich man of the parable sitting before a table and his bags of money. The barn in the background is symbolic of the man's plan to build bigger barns for his grain and goods, so he can relax and say to his soul, "Eat, drink and be merry." The hand of God points toward a bed and a candle. This represents God's words in the parable telling the man that his life is required of him that very night. Jesus uses the parable to urge his listeners to turn away from greed and toward God. (Luke 12:13-34)

"So he set off and went to his father. But while he was still far off, his father saw him and was filled with compassion; he ran and put his arms around him and kissed him."
Luke 15:20

When the Pharisees and the scribes grumble that Jesus receives and eats with sinners, Jesus responds with three parables. All three describe lost things and the joy that results when those things are found. The first parable is about a lost sheep and the shepherd who searches, finds, and rejoices over its recovery. The second parable concerns a lost coin and a woman who sweeps her house until she finds it, and then calls her friends and neighbors to rejoice over its retrieval.

This window depicts the final of the three parables; it is the Parable of the Lost, or Prodigal, Son. After the younger of two sons demands his half of his father's wealth and squanders it all, he comes to realize he is living in far worse circumstances than even his father's servants. He returns to his father prepared to ask humbly for a position as a hired hand. However, the father sees the son coming, and though he is still far off, runs out to meet him, hugging and kissing him to welcome him back. The window shows the ecstatic father's welcome. In the far right is the fatted calf, to be slaughtered for the celebration held in honor of the son's return. In the upper left is the older son, out working in the field. When the elder son hears of his brother's return he is not pleased, and he grumbles with resentment. Yet the father also goes out to this elder brother, asking that he be happy and rejoice in the return of the prodigal, for the younger son was lost but now has been found. (Luke 15:11-32)

"The Pharisee, standing by himself, was praying thus, 'God, I thank you that I am not like other people: thieves, rogues, adulterers, or even like this tax collector.'"
Luke 18:11

The final parable in this window is the parable of the publican and the Pharisee. This parable is about prayer and the proper attitude towards God and others. Jesus tells the parable to individuals who feel superior and view others contemptuously. The

Pharisee, standing to the right, exalts himself in his prayer to God, even going so far as to give thanks that he is not like the nearby tax collector. The illustration even includes the Pharisee pointing a finger at the humble publican. The publican, coming to God in great humility and penitence, kneels with bowed head and outstretched hands, asking God only for mercy. The light, emanating from above, shines upon the head of the tax collector representing the point Jesus is making. It is the publican, coming to God in humility, who leaves the temple justified and lifted up by God. (Luke 18:9-14)

Then an angel from heaven appeared to him and gave him strength.
Luke 22:43

Given that most of the windows in the sanctuary follow a roughly chronological outline, the illustration in the tracery of this window is somewhat out of place. The entire tracery depicts the Garden of Gethsemane after the Last Supper. In this picture from the center of the tracery, Jesus kneels with face upraised and arms extended in a pleading manner. During this night Jesus agonizingly pleads with the Father that the cup he is about to drink might pass from him. Yet, at the same time, Jesus acknowledges that he will surrender his desires to the Father's will. Luke records that an angel from heaven appears to Jesus and strengthens him. In this illustration the artist depicts the angel holding a golden chalice, a characteristic symbol of the Agony in Gethsemane. (Luke 22:39-46)

When he got up from prayer, he came to the disciples and found them sleeping because of grief, and he said to them, "Why are you sleeping? Get up and pray that you may not come into the time of trial."
Luke 22:45-46

After Jesus takes all of the disciples into the Garden of Gethsemane and tells them he is going to pray, he leads Peter and the two sons of Zebedee, James and John, farther into the garden with him. Explaining how distressed and distraught he is, Jesus asks the three to stay and keep watch. However, because of their grief and exhaustion, they keep falling asleep. Three times Jesus returns to them, and each time they are sleeping. The verse of Scripture in the window comes from the gospel of Matthew and records Jesus' words to the disciples the first time he returns to find them sleeping. (Matthew 26:36-46, Mark 14:32-42, Luke 22:45-46)

So Judas brought a detachment of soldiers together with police from the chief priests and the Pharisees, and they came there with lanterns and torches and weapons.
John 18:3

 While Jesus prays to the Father and the disciples sorrowfully sleep, a crowd armed with swords and clubs follows Judas to the Garden of Gethsemane, intent upon seizing and arresting Jesus. (Matthew 26:47, Mark 14:43, Luke 22:47, John 18:3)

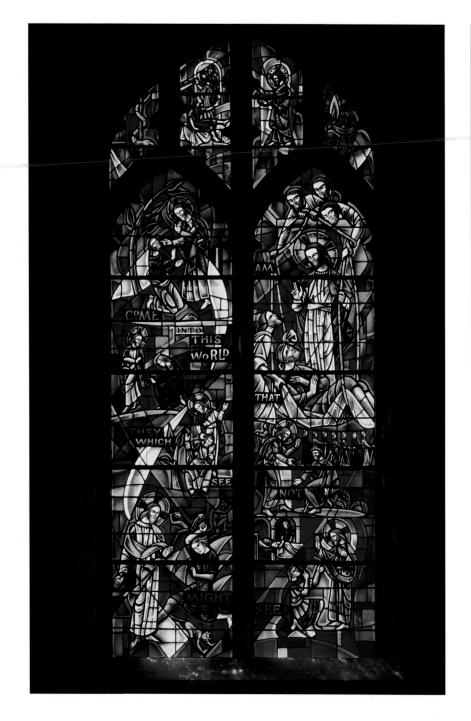

JESUS HEALING

…I am come into this world, that they which see not might see;…
John 9:39b

This window details eight healings that Jesus performs. The large vignette in the right lancet portrays Jesus healing the paralytic, lowered through the roof by four men of faith. Below the paralytic's bed, the window depicts the healing of the ten lepers and the thankfulness of the Samaritan among them. The bottom of this lancet shows the healing of the centurion's servant. In the bottom left lancet Jesus casts out demons, and above that Jesus heals a deaf-mute. Up and to the left is the woman with a hemorrhage touching the hem of Jesus' cloak. The top of the left lancet portrays one of Jesus' Sabbath day miracles, the creation of sight in the man born blind. The eighth healing, in the center of the tracery, illustrates the restoration of life to Jairus's daughter.

The healings happen in a variety of circumstances: in front of large crowds, as with the paralytic and the woman with the hemorrhage; privately with just a few onlookers, as with Jairus's daughter and the blind man; and completely out of sight of others, as with the deaf-mute. In each situation, Jesus demonstrates his power to heal and to bring people out of fear and into faith.

The right tracery pane reveals a lighted lamp topped with a cross, symbolic of Jesus as the light of the world. The left tracery pane shows the serpent on a staff. As Moses saved the lives of the Israelites by lifting up the staff in the wilderness, Jesus, by dying on a cross, will bring eternal life to those who believe in him.

The Scripture in the window is from Jesus' words to the man, born blind, whom he heals on the Sabbath.

Just then some men came, carrying a paralyzed man on a bed. They were trying to bring him in and lay him before Jesus; but finding no way to bring him in because of the crowd, they went up on the roof and let him down with his bed through the tiles into the middle of the crowd in front of Jesus.
Luke 5:18-19

Home in Capernaum, Jesus begins to draw a large crowd of people, many wishing to be healed. In fact, four men carrying a paralytic on his pallet are unable to find entry into the crowded house where Jesus is teaching and healing. Climbing upon the roof they open up a way between the tiles and lower the paralytic in front of Jesus. Seeing their faith, Jesus forgives the man's sins, calling him "my son" in two gospels and "friend" in a third. As three of the men hold ropes from above, the fourth assists from the ground. Jesus, looking intently and compassionately into the paralytic's face, holds up his hand in the symbolic position of blessing as he forgives the man's sins.

This display disturbs the watching scribes and Pharisees who are among the crowd. Understanding their agitation, Jesus heals the man's paralysis in order to display that he does indeed have authority to forgive sins. The response from the onlookers is amazement and awe as well as an outpouring of praise and glory to God. (Matthew 9:1-8, Mark 2:1-12, Luke 5:17-26)

When he entered Capernaum, a centurion came to him, appealing to him and saying, "Lord, my servant is lying at home paralyzed, in terrible distress."
Matthew 8:5-6

In Capernaum a centurion, a Roman captain of 100 men, approaches Jesus, asking him to heal his servant. The centurion kneels at Jesus' feet with humility as he asks for the healing of his servant. The suffering slave lies on a bed in the left corner as someone tends him. The centurion's understanding of Jesus' authority to heal at just a word, without the necessity of his coming to the centurion's home, prompts Jesus to marvel at the Roman soldier's faith. Jesus praises the centurion's belief, and the servant is healed that very hour. (Matthew 8:5-13, Luke 7:1-10)

Then the demons came out of the man.
Luke 8:33a

In this healing of a demoniac, Jesus stands close to the possessed person writhing in torment. This healing could be representative of any number of occasions on which Jesus cast out demons during his ministry. The multiple demons, two pictured in green and a third portrayed in purple, could indicate that this is the healing of the Gerasene

75

demoniac, whom Jesus healed by sending the legion of demons which possessed him into a herd of nearby swine. However, the clothes and the apparent youth of the possessed person could indicate that this is the boy brought to Jesus by his father. It is during this healing, which the disciples were unable to perform, that Jesus explains that the healing could only come about through faith (Matthew 17:20) and much prayer (Mark 9:29). It is also possible, although somewhat improbable, that this vignette illustrates the healing of Mary Magdalene. Scripture explains that she had seven demons cast out of her, but the account of the healing is not detailed.

Regardless of which particular healing this vignette intends to represent, Jesus did perform many healing miracles among those called demon-possessed by Scripture. As this healing so poignantly illustrates, Jesus draws near to them in love and compassion and values them as individuals regardless of their situation. (Matthew 8:28-34, 17:14-18; Mark 5:1-20, 9:14-29, 16:9; Luke 8:2, 8:26-39, 9:38-42)

Then suddenly a woman who had been suffering from hemorrhages for twelve years came up behind him and touched the fringe of his cloak, for she said to herself, "If I only touch his cloak, I will be made well."
Matthew 9:20-21

A woman suffering with a hemorrhage touches the hem of Jesus' cloak, believing even that small contact with him will make her well. Jesus turns back, looking for the recipient of the healing power that he is conscious has gone out from him. He has this awareness although the crowds are pressing in on him from every side. After the woman fearfully confesses that she touched him, Jesus compassionately blesses her with peace and calls her "daughter," explaining that her faith has made her well. This healing takes place as Jesus is on his way to the home of Jairus, a temple official, because Jairus's only daughter is gravely ill. (Matthew 9:19-22, Mark 5:24-34, Luke 8:43-48)

He took her by the hand and said to her, "Talitha cum," which means, "Little girl, get up!" And immediately the girl got up and began to walk about (she was twelve years of age).
Mark 5:41-42a

The center of the tracery reveals the restoration of Jairus's only daughter. Jesus departs for the home of Jairus, a synagogue leader, after the beseeching pleas of Jairus. However, before they can even arrive at the house, news comes to Jesus and the alarmed father that the girl is already dead. Jesus instructs the father to not be afraid, but to only believe. Although mourning has already begun for the girl and the crowd of people by the house scornfully laughs when Jesus says she is only sleeping, the father continues on inside with Jesus, Peter, James, John, and the girl's mother. In the window illustration Jesus stands on the right calling for the girl to get up. The girl herself rises from her bed as her mother and father watch in amazement. (Matthew 9:18-26, Mark 5:22-43, Luke 8:41-56)

He took him aside in private, away from the crowd, and put his fingers into his ears, and he spat and touched his tongue.
Mark 7:33

Jesus places his fingers into the ears of a deaf man before he spits and touches the man's tongue. The upraised hand of Jesus indicates Jesus' prayer, "Be opened." At this the man is able to both hear and speak clearly. Although Jesus orders those witnessing the man's restored hearing and speech to tell no one, many zealously make known the astounding miracle.
(Matthew 15:29-31, Mark 7:31-37)

When he had said this, he spat on the ground and made mud with the saliva and spread the mud on the man's eyes.
John 9:6

On a Sabbath day in Jerusalem, Jesus' disciples point out a man born blind, asking Jesus who sinned — the man or his parents — that he should be sightless. Jesus' response is three-fold. First, he explains that the blindness is not the result of sin, but rather presents an opportunity for God's work to manifest itself. Second, Jesus identifies himself as the light of the world. Finally, Jesus responds by healing the man's blindness.

In the window vignette, Jesus reaches down to touch the blind man's eyes with one hand. The small pile of dirt between the knees of the blind man and Jesus' foot indicates Jesus made mud to place on the man's eyes. Some of the Pharisees accuse Jesus of failing to keep the Sabbath, as they consider something as simple as making mud to be work and a failure to observe the Sabbath laws. The Pharisees subsequently question both the blind man and his parents. Ultimately, in anger and scorn, they drive the man out of the synagogue.

When Jesus seeks him out after the man's final dispute with the Pharisees, Jesus reveals himself as the Son of Man. The man, previously blind, proclaims his belief in Jesus and worships him, making his kneeling posture in the window particularly appropriate.
(John 9:1-41)

77

"As long as I am in the world, I am the light of the world."
John 9:5

Before Jesus heals the man born blind, he proclaims himself the light of the world. This lamp is a symbol of Jesus, the light of the world. (John 9:5)

Then one of them, when he saw that he was healed, turned back, praising God with a loud voice. He prostrated himself at Jesus' feet and thanked him. And he was a Samaritan.
Luke 17:15-16

When ten lepers, standing at a distance, call out to Jesus to heal them, Jesus instructs them to go show themselves to the priests. As they obediently go on their way, their leprosy apparently disappears. Yet, only one turns back in gratitude. The one, a Samaritan, praises God and falls at Jesus' feet, thanking him. Robe-clad men, representing the other nine lepers, march across the background of this illustration. The tenth man kneels in grateful thanks before Jesus. As in each of these illustrations of healing, Jesus' upraised hand proclaims a blessing available to all who have belief and faith. (Luke 17:11-19)

78

"And just as Moses lifted up the serpent in the wilderness, so must the Son of Man be lifted up, that whoever believes in him may have eternal life."
John 3:14-15

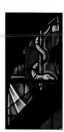

The serpent on a staff is a symbol of Jesus' crucifixion because Jesus compares Moses lifting up the brazen serpent in the wilderness to Jesus himself being "lifted up". A similar serpent and staff image is contained in the Moses window and symbolizes the events enumerated in Numbers chapter 21. An onslaught of fiery serpents causes many to die, but those who look at the bronze serpent recover. Here the serpent and staff indicate both Jesus' intermediate gift of healing as well as the ultimate gift of eternal life for all who believe. (Numbers 21:5-9, John 3:14-15)

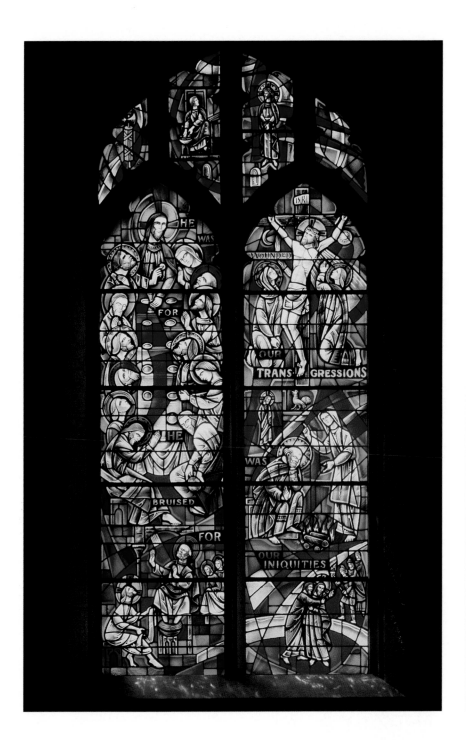

THE PASSION

...he was wounded for our transgressions, he was bruised for our iniquities:
Isaiah 53:5a

This verse from Isaiah, foretelling a suffering servant who will bear the punishment for human sin, is a most appropriate theme for this window depicting Christ's passion. In his time of public ministry, Jesus showed himself to be the Lord and Teacher, the Master. Yet, as the lower left of the window portrays, he knelt to wash the feet of his disciples in an attitude of service, assuming the position of a lowly servant.

Above, Jesus eats the Last Supper with his disciples. In a matter of hours, he himself will become the sacrificial Passover lamb, the ultimate atonement that saves us from death.

He is bruised and wounded by the beating of the guards, scourged by the orders of Pilate, and pierced by a spear to verify his death. By enduring this misery, he bore the sin of all. The window highlights some of those sins. Judas, in the bottom right lancet, reveals love of wealth and power above love of God and others, as well as complete betrayal. Just above Judas, Peter manifests reluctance to obey and denial of Jesus. Jesus took upon himself even the sin of Pontius Pilate, portrayed in the tracery washing his hands, who allowed the crucifixion because he feared the crowd.

This ultimate act of love on the part of God, the willing sacrifice of Jesus Christ, God's only Son, manifests God's sovereign plan for the redemption of mankind.

Jesus answered, "You do not know now what I am doing, but later you will understand."
John 13:7

Jesus, seated and holding a towel, prepares to wash Peter's feet at the Last Supper. Peter raises his hands to indicate his resistance to the Lord doing such a dirty and menial task as two other disciples look on from the table. Jesus performs this service for his disciples as an example they are to emulate. They are to serve one another in humility, and in doing so they will be blessed. (John 13:1-20)

After saying this Jesus was troubled in spirit, and declared, "Very truly, I tell you, one of you will betray me."
John 13:21

Jesus, sitting at the head of the table, shares the Last Supper with all twelve disciples. It is at this meal that Jesus talks about his upcoming betrayal, illustrates the breaking of his body, and speaks of his blood being shed for the forgiveness of sins. Judas sits to the right, at the foot of the table, reaching for the moneybag for which he is responsible. The moneybag serves as a reminder that Judas has already arranged to deliver Jesus to the chief priests

for thirty pieces of silver. Judas's role as the betrayer also explains why a halo is not present around his head. On the same side of the table, but sitting beside Jesus and leaning toward him, is the Apostle John, portrayed as a beardless youth. (Matthew 26:20-29, Mark 14:17-25, Luke 22:14-23, John 13:12-29)

[Judas] approached Jesus to kiss him; but Jesus said to him, "Judas, is it with a kiss that you are betraying the Son of Man?"
Luke 22:47b-48

Judas reaches out to kiss Jesus as a signal to the multitude he has led out to the Garden of Gethsemane. The three men to the right are representative of the band of Roman soldiers and the chief priests, scribes, and elders of the Jewish people that Judas brought to Jesus that they might arrest him. (Matthew 26:47-50, Mark 14:43-46, Luke 22:47-48, John 18:1-3)

Then a servant-girl, seeing him in the firelight, stared at him and said, "This man also was with him." But he denied it, saying, "Woman, I do not know him." Luke 22:56-57

Simon Peter sits by the fire in the courtyard of the high priest. Peter's hand is raised in denial as the servant girl maintains that he is a follower of Jesus of Nazareth. The cock in the top of this vignette represents Jesus' prophecy that Peter would deny him three times before the cock crowed. Jesus gazes at Peter from the left corner in a poignant reminder that the Lord actually turned and looked at Peter immediately after his third denial. (Matthew 26:69-75, Mark 14:66-72, Luke 22:54-62, John 18:15-27)

So when Pilate saw that he could do nothing, but rather that a riot was beginning, he took some water and washed his hands before the crowd, saying, "I am innocent of this man's blood; see to it yourselves."
Matthew 27:24

In the center of the tracery, Jesus stands bound before Pontius Pilate, Roman governor of Judea. Pilate washes his hands in an attempt to demonstrate his innocence in Jesus' crucifixion. Although Pilate recognizes envy as the motivation behind the chief priests' desire for Jesus' death, and although Pilate's wife pleads with him to spare the life of Jesus because of a dream, Pilate succumbs to the crowd's demand for Jesus' crucifixion. When he feels his position is threatened, Pilate consents to Jesus' death. In the left pane, a *fasces* of the *lictor*, an ax bound with rods which was carried before the chief magistrate by an attendant (*lictor*) in ancient Rome, is a typical symbol of the Roman government. The symbol suggests both the power of Rome and Pilate's declaration to Jesus that he held the power to either release or crucify him. (Matthew 27:11-26; Mark 15:1-15; Luke 23:1-7, 13-25; John 18:28 -19:16)

When Jesus saw his mother and the disciple whom he loved standing beside her, he said to his mother, "Woman, here is your son."
John 19:26

Jesus hangs dying on the cross. At the top of the cross the inscription *INRI* appears. This is the Latin abbreviation of "Jesus of Nazareth, King of the Jews," the inscription put on the cross by Pilate. The moon to the left and the sun to the right suggest the three-hour period when the sun darkened. Mary, the mother of Jesus, kneels on the left of the cross, and the beloved disciple John looks on from the right. Jesus requests that John take responsibility for Mary and they be as mother and son. Even in the midst of agony, Jesus' concern is for the people that he loves. (Matthew 27:33-56, Mark 15:22-41, Luke 23:33-49, John 19:17-30)

ACTS OF THE APOSTLES

…ye shall receive power, after that the Holy Ghost is come upon you: and ye shall be witnesses unto me,…
Acts 1:8a

God clearly manifests sovereignty in both history and redemption by sending the Holy Spirit. Across the tracery, the Holy Spirit descends upon the believers gathered for the Jewish day of Pentecost. The Holy Spirit, symbolized by a dove and tongues of fire, falls upon both men and women. The Holy Spirit empowers the disciples to preach the gospel, make and baptize disciples, and teach. They undertake this mission immediately, first preaching to the Jews in Jerusalem and then spreading the gospel to Samaria. The center left lancet represents the Holy Spirit coming upon these converts. The good news spreads farther as Philip converts and baptizes the Ethiopian eunuch, shown in the top left lancet, and Peter spreads the gospel to the Gentiles, shown in the top right.

The power of the Spirit is also present with the disciples as they suffer and endure persecution and imprisonment. Some, like James, die a martyr's death, while others, such as Peter, miraculously escape. The bottom right lancet reflects James' martyrdom, while just above, an angel leads Peter safely out of prison.

The last recorded act of the apostles before the Holy Spirit comes upon them is the replacement of Judas with Matthias. The lower left lancet illustrates the disciples choosing between Matthias and Justus.

82

And they cast lots for them, and the lot fell on Matthias; and he was added to the eleven apostles.
Acts 1:26

Before the descent of the Holy Spirit at Pentecost, the disciples determine to replace Judas. Justus and Matthias are put forward, both having been with the disciples from the time of the baptism of John through Jesus' resurrection. The apostles pray that God will direct them by the casting of lots. Matthias is chosen and added, and is seen in the upper left with the book and battle-ax symbol above his head. Matthias's symbols also appear in the wood carving around the Chancel window; they represent his missionary endeavors and his ultimate beheading. (Acts 1:12-26)

Divided tongues, as of fire, appeared among them, and a tongue rested on each of them.
Acts 2:3

The middle of the tracery features a dove, symbolizing the Holy Spirit. Flames shower across all four of the tracery windows, while the disciples each have a tongue of fire resting upon them. Scripture says "they were all together," probably meaning a large group of believers, possibly numbering over one hundred. Both men and women are represented in this vignette of the baptism by the Holy Spirit. (Acts 2:1-42)

Then Peter and John laid their hands on them, and they received the Holy Spirit.
Acts 8:17

After the persecution that arises following the stoning of Stephen (see the Chancel Window), Philip preaches in Samaria where many believe and are baptized. However, the Holy Spirit is not yet given to the Samaritan converts. The apostles send Peter and John to the new believers in Samaria. When Peter and John arrive they pray that the Samaritans might receive the Holy Spirit, and they lay hands on them. The Holy Spirit is given and received, signified by the dove. (Acts 8:4-25)

He commanded the chariot to stop, and both of them, Philip and the eunuch, went down into the water, and Philip baptized him. Acts 8:38

Philip baptizes the Ethiopian eunuch after explaining the gospel of Jesus to him, using the Old Testament book of Isaiah as a starting place. This represents the spread of the gospel to a

83

different race and a far country, as well as the proliferation of the gospel by means of explaining Scripture. (Acts 8:26-40)

[Peter] saw the heaven opened and something like a large sheet coming down, being lowered to the ground by its four corners. In it were all kinds of four-footed creatures and reptiles and birds of the air. Acts 10:11-12

Cornelius, in the tower on the right, is a prayerful and God-fearing Gentile centurion. Because of his prayers and alms, he has a vision in which an angel instructs him to send for Peter. Cornelius sends three men to Joppa to search out Peter. As they approach the city, Peter climbs upon the roof to pray. As Peter prays, he has his own vision. He sees animals, both clean and unclean, lowered from the sky. These two visions prompt the eventual conversion of Cornelius, his relatives, and close friends, as well as their baptism by the Holy Spirit. It also leads to the full acceptance of Gentile converts into the faith. Peter's vision of the clean and unclean animals also becomes a foundation for the removal of Jewish dietary laws for believers in Christ, building upon Jesus' own words. (Matthew 15:10-20, Mark 7:14-19, Acts 10:1-11:18)

[King Herod] had James, the brother of John, killed with the sword.
Acts 12:2

James, the brother of John, is arrested by King Herod, the grandson of Herod the Great, who ruled at the time of Jesus' birth. James is the first of the apostles martyred for their faith. The death of James apparently pleases the Jews and encourages Herod to make more arrests. (Acts 12:1-3)

The angel said to him, "Fasten your belt and put on your sandals." He did so. Then he said to him, "Wrap your cloak around you and follow me."
Acts 12:8

Because of the favorable response Herod received from the arrest and death of James, Herod arrests Peter. However, on the night before his execution, an angel of the Lord frees Peter from prison, escorting him outside the city. Peter immediately finds the church praying for him at the house of John Mark and relates his miraculous escape. After instructing them to spread word of his rescue, he leaves Jerusalem for another place. (Acts 12:3-19)

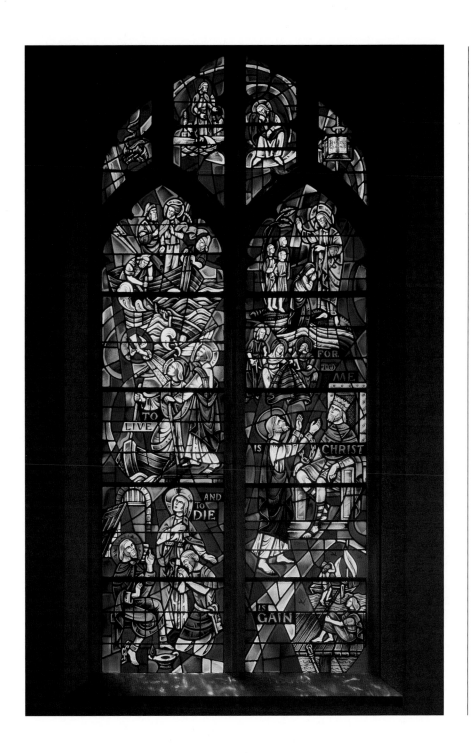

PAUL

For to me to live is Christ, and to die is gain.
Philippians 1:21

The verse in the window, from Paul's letter to the Philippians, emphasizes Christ, and places Paul as the secondary figure in his own life. The illustrations within this window primarily portray Paul's life as Christ's apostle and the dangers he undertakes in following the resurrected Jesus.

The portraits of Paul's life begin in the bottom of the right lancet. Saul, as he was known in his youth, sits in contemplation on a dock in Tarsus, the town of his birth. Continuing clockwise, Paul proclaims the gospel to his jailer. Above this scene, Paul embarks on one of his missionary voyages, while a dove, symbolizing the Holy Spirit, flies overhead.

On numerous occasions, Paul almost dies from his evangelical endeavors. The top of the left lancet illustrates the shipwreck Paul encounters as a prisoner on the way to Rome. The left tracery panel pictures the poisonous viper that bites Paul after that same shipwreck.

Through Paul's preaching, the gospel spreads to Europe. The tracery reveals the vision that calls Paul to Macedonia. The last tracery symbol is the one most common for Paul. The sword of the Spirit and the word of God reflect Paul's passion for proclaiming Christ in all situations. Paul's baptism of Lydia, top right lancet, marks the first European convert to Christianity.

Below, Paul works as a tentmaker with Priscilla and Aquila to support himself and his missionary endeavors. The final picture shows Paul in chains as he pleads with King Agrippa, not for his freedom, but for the King's own salvation through Jesus Christ.

85

"I am a Jew, born in Tarsus in Cilicia,..."
Acts 22:3a

Saul, a Roman citizen, sits on a dock of Tarsus, the city of his birth. Saul, of the tribe of Benjamin, was born to Hebrew parents who properly circumcised him on the eighth day and had him trained in the Law of Moses. Brought up in Jerusalem, Saul was educated in the law by Gamaliel, a teacher of the law very highly regarded by the Jewish people of the day. Saul became a Pharisee. Indeed, he was most zealous for God, even to the point of persecuting, arresting, and testifying against believers in Christ. However, his encounter with the risen Christ, on the Damascus road, changes his life forever. For a description of that experience, see the Chancel Window section. (Acts 9:11, 22:3-5; Philippians 3:4-6)

So, being sent out by the Holy Spirit, they went down to Seleucia; and from there they sailed to Cyprus.
Acts 13:4

Saul, commonly identified by his Roman name, Paul, stands on a dock. He and Barnabas are ready to embark upon Paul's first missionary journey. The two are leaving Antioch, where they have been teaching Christian disciples for a year. While worshiping and fasting, the prophets and teachers of the Antioch church receive instructions from the Holy Spirit: they are to send Barnabas and Saul out to do the work of the Lord.

During this missionary voyage, Paul and Barnabas initially proclaim the word of God in the synagogues, primarily to Jews. However, during one particular stop, in Pisidian Antioch, the majority of Jews not only refuse to believe in Jesus Christ, but they also incite the powerful Jews of the area to stir up persecution against Paul and Barnabas. As a result, Paul and Barnabas increasingly turn to the Gentiles with their missionary endeavors. Repeatedly, in numerous cities, both Jews and Gentiles come to faith in Jesus, while at the same time those who do not believe stir up violent opposition to Paul and Barnabas. (Acts 11:19-26, 13:1-14:28)

During the night Paul had a vision: there stood a man of Macedonia pleading with him and saying, "Come over to Macedonia and help us."
Acts 16:9

After returning to Antioch with Barnabas and staying there for a considerable period with the disciples, Paul desires to return and visit the brothers in the towns of his first missionary journey. A dispute arises between Paul and Barnabas over John Mark, so Barnabas leaves for Cyprus with John Mark and Paul goes in the opposite direction with Silas. This second missionary journey takes Paul through Syria, Cilicia, Derbe, and Lystra. In Lystra, Paul meets and includes the young man Timothy. After Paul travels through Phrygia and Galatia, the Holy Spirit repeatedly bars him from entering various cities in the province of Asia and in Bythinia. Denied the opportunity to preach the gospel, Paul ventures down into Troas.

While in Troas, Paul finally receives a call in a vision. During the night, Paul sees a man of Macedonia beseeching him for help. Immediately Paul and his cohorts leave for Macedonia, traveling from Troas to Samothrace, then on to Neapolis, and finally to Philippi, a Roman colony and the leading city of that district of Macedonia. In this way, Paul enters Europe for the first time. (Acts 16:1-12)

When [Lydia] and her household were baptized, she urged us, saying, "If you have judged me to be faithful to the Lord, come and stay at my home."
Acts 16:15a

Paul's first stop in Macedonia is Philippi. Thinking he will find a place of prayer by the river, Paul sets out on his first Sabbath in Philippi hoping to find it. Discovering only women at the place of prayer does not deter him. Rather, he begins to proclaim the gospel to them. Lydia of Thyatira is there by the river. She is a worshiper of God and a dealer in purple cloth. When she hears Paul's message, she believes and has Paul baptize her, along with her household. Afterwards, she implores Paul and his companions to stay with her at her home. This is Paul's first convert in Europe, interestingly originating from the same place, Asia, where the

Spirit would not previously allow him to go. (Acts 16:13-15)

The jailer called for lights, and rushing in, he fell down trembling before Paul and Silas.
Acts 16:29

Still in Philippi, Paul continues to proclaim the word of the Lord in the place of prayer. During these days, a slave-girl with a spirit of divination trails after Paul shouting about God and salvation. After many days, Paul commands the spirit to leave her. The owners of the slave-girl see that the spirit, and their opportunity to profit from it, is gone so they turn on Paul and his companion Silas. Because of the accusations of the slave's owners, Paul and Silas receive a flogging and imprisonment.

Refusing to despair, Paul and Silas instead sing hymns and pray within the innermost cell of the jail. Late at night, an earthquake occurs that causes all the prisoners to be freed. The jailer, knowing he will be condemned if the prisoners escape, fears for his life. When the jailer discovers all the prisoners still inside he is overwhelmed and pleads to Paul and Silas, "What must I do to be saved?" After Paul and Silas explain the word of the Lord to him, he believes and receives baptism along with his entire household.

Paul and Silas are released the next day, and before they leave Philippi, they meet with the brothers at Lydia's house and encourage them. (Acts 16:16-34)

Paul went to see them, and, because he was of the same trade, he stayed with them, and they worked together – by trade they were tentmakers.
Acts 18:2b-3

After leaving Philippi, Paul and Silas preach Christ in Thessalonica for about a month. The result is twofold: some of the Jews, a large number of Greeks, and numerous prominent women believe, while others instigate a riot by the Jews of the city. This forces Paul and Silas to depart for Berea where many Jews and Greeks, both men and women, believe. The Thessalonian Jews arrive in Berea, again agitating and stirring up a crowd, so that Paul goes alone to Athens to escape the tumult. In Athens the numerous idols and the pervasive idol worship greatly distress Paul. After reasoning in the synagogues and preaching in the Areopagus, Paul leaves for Corinth.

Once in Corinth, Paul lives and works with Priscilla and Aquila, the fellow tentmakers pictured above. Each Sabbath in the synagogue he tries to convince the Jews that Jesus is the Messiah. After Silas and Timothy arrive from Macedonia to join him, Paul devotes himself to preaching. The Jews vehemently oppose Paul and his teachings, becoming so abusive that Paul divorces himself from them, declaring that his future missionary endeavors will be toward the Gentiles. Paul stays in Corinth for a year and a half, teaching the word of God at the urging and encouragement of the Lord.

After this period in Corinth, Paul embarks upon his third missionary journey. He leaves for Syria with Priscilla and Aquila; their first stop is Ephesus. After a brief time, Priscilla and Aquila remain there while Paul ventures on to Caesarea, Antioch, and various places in Galatia and Phrygia. Everywhere he goes Paul strengthens and encourages the disciples. Returning to Ephesus, Paul stays there three years, eventually using a lecture hall to proclaim the gospel of God's grace. (Acts 18:1-11)

Agrippa said to Paul, "You have permission to speak for yourself." Then Paul stretched out his hand and began to defend himself.
Acts 26:1

Paul's missionary efforts continue as he travels throughout Greece. As Paul heads to Jerusalem in order to take a gift of money to the saints there, numerous people warn him that severe trouble awaits in Jerusalem.

Indeed, shortly after Paul arrives in Jerusalem, a riot ensues when he goes into the temple to complete a vow. The Jews accuse Paul of preaching an abandonment of Moses and Jewish customs. A Roman commander arrives with his troops, barely rescuing Paul from the crowd wanting to kill him. When the commander orders Paul flogged and questioned, Paul asserts his Roman citizenship, alarming the commander and causing him to withdraw the orders.

Another uproar results after the Sanhedrin question Paul. The Jews plan an ambush of Paul, but when their plan is discovered, the commander safely removes Paul to Caesarea and the Governor, Felix.

Although no charges are proven against Paul, Governor Felix keeps him under guard for two years.

When Felix is succeeded by Festus, the Jewish leaders use that opportunity to again present their charges against Paul. Hoping Governor Festus will transfer Paul to Jerusalem, they again plan an ambush. However, Festus insists they present any charges against Paul in Caesarea. The Jews from Jerusalem bring the charges against Paul; however, they cannot prove them. And Paul, unwilling to go to Jerusalem to stand trial on the matter, appeals to Caesar.

This appeal to Caesar keeps Paul under arrest and sets up the pictured meeting with King Agrippa. When King Agrippa arrives to pay his respects to the newly installed Governor Festus, his curiosity is aroused by Festus's news of Paul. Agrippa asks to hear Paul for himself.

Paul states his defense to King Agrippa. However, more than defending himself, Paul makes a plea for the conversion of all present. Both Governor Festus and King Agrippa agree that Paul is innocent of anything that would require death or imprisonment; but because Paul appealed to Caesar, to Caesar and Rome he must go. (Acts 25:23-26:32)

Paul said to the centurion and the soldiers, "Unless these men stay in the ship, you cannot be saved." Then the soldiers cut away the ropes of the boat and set it adrift. Acts 27:31-32

When Paul is sent as a prisoner to Rome, Luke, the subsequent writer of Acts, and another friend go with him. They travel on a ship with two hundred seventy six aboard, including soldiers and other prisoners. After almost six tortuous months on board the ship, a storm strikes — one so terrible that the crew fears for its life. Paul, here shown speaking to the centurion, urges everyone to stay onboard. In the midst of the terrible storm that eventually shipwrecks them on the island of Malta, Paul assures everyone on the boat that God has told him through an angel that no loss of life will occur. (Acts 27:1-44)

Paul had gathered a bundle of brushwood and was putting it on the fire, when a viper, driven out by the heat, fastened itself on his hand. Acts 28:3

The island on which they shipwreck is Malta. As Paul is putting gathered brushwood on a fire after they wash ashore, a viper bites him. When Paul survives with no ill effects, the natives of Malta begin to say that he is a god. The shipwrecked group is warmly welcomed into the chief official's home and hosted for three days. While there, Paul heals the official's father. This, as well as Paul's subsequent healings of other islanders, creates such good will that the people honor Paul, and all his needs are met for the three months they remain on the island. (Acts 28:1-10)

Take the helmet of salvation, and the sword of the Spirit, which is the word of God. Ephesians 6:17

The most commonly used symbol for the Apostle Paul is the cross-hilted sword behind an open Bible with the words *Spiritus Gladius,* Latin for "Sword of the Spirit," written across the open pages. (Ephesians 6:17)

THE REVELATION

I am Alpha and Omega, the beginning and the end(ing),…
What thou seest, write in a book, and send it unto the seven churches…
Revelation 1:8a & 1:11b

The focus of this window is two-fold as highlighted by the choice of Scripture. The first theme is the symbolic description of Jesus Christ. Jesus dominates the left lancet and symbols of John's vision surround the Christ. A golden lampstand, stars, the keys of Death and Hades, lightning, a rainbow, and the two-edged sword all reflect what John sees of the throne room of God. The four images in the tracery — the Greek letter *alpha*, the Lamb of God, the twenty-four crowns and the Greek letter *omega* — are a part of the vision of the throne room of God.

The second theme is that of John writing to seven specific churches in the province of Asia as Jesus commands. In the top of the right lancet, John obediently writes in a book all that God chooses to reveal. Seven angels, each representing one of the churches, along with depictions of the churches, make up the remainder of the window.

"I am the Alpha and the Omega," says the Lord God, who is and who was and who is to come, the Almighty.
Revelation 1:8

The Greek letters *alpha* and *omega* (the first and last letters of the Greek alphabet) are shown on either side of the tracery. The book of Revelation uses the name "Alpha and Omega" four times to emphasize that God is eternal and omnipotent. "I am the first and the last" is also used to refer to God in Isaiah 44:6.

In Revelation, "Alpha and Omega" is first used for identity; second in command to John, to write what he is about to see and send it to the seven churches in Asia; third in promise that God will give freely from the fountain of life; and finally in assurance that Jesus will come and reward everyone according to his or her work. (Isaiah 44:6; Revelation 1:8, 11-20, 21:6, 22:12-13)

I was in the spirit on the Lord's day, and I heard behind me a loud voice like a trumpet saying, "Write in a book what you see and send it to the seven churches, ..."
Revelation 1:10-11a

John, during his exile on the island of Patmos, sits and writes in a book as instructed by Jesus Christ. (Revelation 1:9-11)

And in the midst of the lampstands I saw one like the Son of Man, clothed with a long robe and with a golden sash across his chest. In his right hand he held seven stars, and from his mouth came a sharp, two-edged sword, and his face was like the sun shining with full force.
Revelation 1:13 & 16

This illustration of Jesus on the throne depicts numerous symbols from the Revelation to John. Jesus sits enthroned, holding in his right hand the stars with a seven-torch lampstand below his feet. The symbolic keys of Death and Hades hang on his right, and a two-edged sword comes from his mouth. Around the throne are the rainbow and the lightning of chapter four. (Revelation 1:12-20, 4:1-5)

91

"To the angel of the church in Ephesus write: ..."
"And to the angel of the church in Smyrna write: "
"And to the angel of the church in Pergamum write:" Revelation 2:1a, 8a, 12a

John is first commanded to write to the angels of Ephesus, Smyrna, and Pergamos (KJV). Banners flow across the angels, proclaiming their cities. Two angels hold very modern-looking church buildings. All three gaze upward towards the enthroned Jesus Christ. (Revelation 2:1-17)

"And to the angel of the church in Thyatira write: These are the words of the Son of God, ... And to the angel of the church in Sardis write: These are the words of him who has the seven spirits of God and the seven stars."
Revelation 2:18a, 3:1a

Thyatira and Sardis are addressed next by the writings of John. Thyatira is both praised and chastised, while Sardis is called to repent and obey the gospel previously preached. A few persons in Sardis are commended, but not by name. (Revelation 2:18-3:6)

"And to the angel of the church in Philadelphia write: These are the words of the holy one, the true one, who has the key of David, who opens and no one will shut, who shuts and no one opens. ... And to the angel of the church in Laodicea write: The words of the Amen, the faithful and true witness, the origin of God's creation."
Revelation 3:7 & 14

The letter to the church of Philadelphia is full of praise for the community of faith there; although they have little power, they have kept the Lord's word and have not denied his name. Laodicea is severely reproved for being lukewarm, having become apathetic because of their material wealth. (Revelation 3:7-22)

Around the throne are twenty-four thrones, and seated on the thrones are twenty-four elders, dressed in white robes, with golden crowns on their heads.
Revelation 4:4

Twenty-four crowns, representing the elders around the Lord's throne, are shown here in the tracery and can also be seen in the woodcarvings within the Chancel window. (Revelation 4:4-11)

They sing a new song: "You are worthy to take the scroll and to open its seals, for you were slaughtered and by your blood you ransomed for God saints from every tribe and language and people and nation."
Revelation 5:9

Jesus Christ is the Lamb of God. In the tracery, the Lamb of God, or *Agnus Dei*, stands on the book of the seven seals. The *Agnus Dei* is one of the most ancient Christian symbols. (Revelation 5:1-6:1)

THE CHANCEL WINDOW

… this do in remembrance of me.
Luke 22:19b, I Corinthians 11:24b

The sculpted gold Chancel window is designed to function either lit, as shown, or unlit, in which case the gold relief stands out against a dark background. Henry Willet, of Willet Stained Glass Studios, the creators of our windows, first developed this technique. Marguerite Gaudin, the designer of all our large sanctuary windows, designed the first window that utilized this technique.

This window focuses on two themes. The primary emphasis is on the resurrection and ascension of Jesus Christ. The second theme is discipleship.

At the bottom of the center section, an angel at the tomb tells the three women that Jesus is not there. On either side of the empty tomb panel, Jesus appears to Mary Magdalene and Thomas, who kneel at his feet.

In the middle of the center section, Jesus gives the Great Commission. Above that, in the top center panel, is Jesus' triumphal ascension into heaven.

The remaining four vignettes represent various disciples. Peter and John heal the man at the Gate Beautiful, Stephen is stoned, Saul is struck blind on the road to Damascus, and Dorcas exemplifies good works for the poor.

At the bottom of the window, below the scene at the tomb, are the symbols of baptism and communion. The symbols of our two sacraments surround a *vesica piscis* aureole, which in turn frames the freestanding silver and ebony cross.

But he said to them, "Do not be alarmed; you are looking for Jesus of Nazareth, who was crucified. He has been raised; he is not here."
Mark 16:6a

Mary Magdalene kneels in the foreground. Mary (the mother of James) and Salome stand on the far side of the open, empty tomb. One of the women holds a jar of spice, brought to anoint the body of Jesus. An angel, wings spread, tells them not to be afraid, that Jesus is not there but has risen. The drape of fabric on the edge of the tomb represents the grave clothes Jesus left behind.
(Matthew 28:5-8, Mark 16:1-7, Luke 24:1-10)

Jesus said to her, "Mary!" She turned and said to him in Hebrew, "Rabbouni!" (which means Teacher).
John 20:16

The apostles Peter and John, having found the tomb empty, leave Mary Magdalene alone. Mary weeps, grieving that Jesus is dead, and that his body is gone as well. As she weeps, she notices a man. Believing him to be the gardener, she asks if he has taken Jesus' body. When the man calls her by name, she recognizes him. It is Jesus. The flower behind her back and the tree overhead suggest her initial mistake of thinking Jesus is the gardener. Jesus' raised hand signifies his statement that she should not cling to him, as he has not yet ascended. (John 20:14-18)

Then he said to Thomas, "Put your finger here and see my hands. Reach out your hand and put it in my side. Do not doubt but believe."
John 20:27

Thomas, having missed the appearance of Jesus to the disciples on that first evening after the resurrection, rashly says he will not believe until he sees and touches the resurrected Jesus. Although Thomas must wait eight long days, Jesus does appear again. Speaking directly to Thomas, Jesus implores him to touch and see the reality of his resurrected body. Thomas responds with a cry of faith, "My Lord and my God."
(John 20:24-31)

95

"Go therefore and make disciples of all nations, baptizing them in the name of the Father and of the Son and of the Holy Spirit, and teaching them to

obey everything that I have commanded you."
Matthew 28:19-20a

On a mountain in Galilee, Jesus gives his disciples the instructions that we call the Great Commission. The walking sticks held in the hands of some of the disciples indicate Jesus' command that they "go". The scallop shell positioned between Jesus' right hand and nimbus corresponds to the decree to baptize. The instruction to teach is represented by the book held in the arms of the disciple in the forefront. (Matthew 28:16-20)

When [Jesus] had said this, as they were watching, he was lifted up, and a cloud took him out of their sight. Acts 1:9

The disciples gaze in wonder as Jesus ascends to heaven. Before Jesus leaves them, he instructs them to remain in Jerusalem. He promises them power when the Holy Spirit comes upon them. Two angels flank Jesus, perhaps representative of the two men in white robes who speak to the disciples after the ascension. (Luke 24:44-53, Acts 1:4-11)

Peter looked intently at him, as did John, and said, "Look at us." And he fixed his attention on them, expecting to receive something from them. Acts 3:4-5

A lame man at the Beautiful Gate of the temple begs for alms as the people of Jerusalem enter for the hour of prayer. When Peter and John stop before him he expects to receive alms, but his expectations are far exceeded when he is healed in the name of Jesus Christ of Nazareth. (Acts 3:1-11)

Then they dragged [Stephen] out of the city and began to stone him; and the witnesses laid their coats at the feet of a young man named Saul. Acts 7:58

Stephen gazes into heaven and sees Jesus at God's right hand. Saul, supporting both the persecution of Christians and the stoning of Stephen, stands in the left corner holding the coats of those stoning Stephen. (Acts 6:8-8:1)

He fell to the ground and heard a voice saying to him, "Saul, Saul, why do you persecute me?" Acts 9:4

After receiving authorization from the head priest, Saul heads toward Damascus to arrest any believers. He is murderously intent on discovering and persecuting followers of the Way, as the early Christians were called. However, Saul's life completely changes when he encounters the ascended Jesus on the road to Damascus. Saul's horse rears in the right corner, and light from heaven falls upon Saul as he encounters the living Christ, visible in the top left corner. (Acts 9:1-9, 22:4-11, 26:12-15)

Now in Joppa there was a disciple whose name was Tabitha, which in Greek is Dorcas. She was devoted to good works and acts of charity.
Acts 9:36

Dorcas, known for her deeds of kindness and service, falls ill and dies. Peter's prayers bring her back to life, but before that occurs, the widows mourning Dorcas show Peter tunics and other clothing that she made. The tunic (pictured in the right corner) and the spool of thread with needle (in the left) represent her life of charity. (Acts 9:36-42)

"This do in remembrance of me."(KJV)
Luke 22:19b

This verse is written in three horizontal bars below the resurrection vignette on either side of the *vesica piscis* aureole. The shape of this aureole recalls the symbolic fish and the rebus obtained from the Greek word for *fish* (ICTHUS) – Jesus Christ, Son of God, Savior. On the right are the symbols of communion – a chalice, stalks of wheat, and a cluster of grapes. Similarly, on the left are symbols of baptism – the serpentine water and fish, the scallop shell, and a dove.
(Luke 22:14-23, Mathew 28:16-20)

WOODCARVINGS

The chancel window also includes numerous woodcarvings. Created by the George Ciukurescu Company of Philadelphia, the woodcarvings depict God and discipleship in symbols.

Installed above the chancel window is an oak carving of the *manus dei*, "the hand of God". The open hand, coming forth from billowing clouds, is an ancient and universal symbol of God the Father. Rays, symbolizing power and might, project from the clouds. The triangle from which the hand emanates represents the Holy Trinity. Finally on either side of the triangle appear the letters *alpha* and *omega*; as the first and last letters of the Greek alphabet, these letters refer to Jesus Christ as the beginning and ending of all things.

Also on the wall, separate from the actual wooden screen within which the stained glass window is set, are plaques on either side of the chancel window. Ten small plaques of messianic roses, five on each side, symbolize the Messiah. The number ten represents order and peace. The six larger plaques, three on each side, signify the attributes of God. Beginning with the top left is the cross and orb, denoting God's power. The crown and laurel of the middle left plaque connote God's majesty. The bottom plaque of a lamp and book symbolizes God's wisdom. The burning heart of the top right plaque indicates God's love. The middle plaque depicts the Ark of the Covenant which denotes the mercy of God, and the final plaque portrays scales, representative of God's justice.

At the top of the screen is the descending dove with a tri-radiant nimbus, representing the Holy Spirit. To the left of the dove is a burning bush. Reminiscent of the call of Moses, the burning bush brings to mind God's presence. Additionally, the Presbyterian Church in the U.S. (the Southern Presbyterian Church), utilized the burning bush symbol on its seal before the Northern and Southern branches reunited to become the Presbyterian Church USA in 1983. On the right of the dove is a ship, symbolic of the church universal. On either side of the window are circular openings holding symbols for each of the final twelve apostles, the original twelve with Judas Escariot excluded and Matthias included. Reading from the top and alternating left to right are crossed keys symbolic of Peter, the cross in the shape of an X for Andrew, a boat hook and fish for Simon the Zealot, and a scallop shell and sword for James the Greater. The typical symbol of a chalice and serpent represents John, three purses signify Matthew, the basket and Tau cross correspond to Philip, and three flaying knives symbolize Bartholomew. A builder's square and spear denote Thomas, the saw indicates the disciple known as James the Less, and the inverted cross, spear and club are symbols of Jude. The Christmas window chapter contains details of the Scripture and legends from which these symbols derive. The final crest of an open Bible and battle-ax refers to Matthias and is also found, and more fully explained, in the chapter on the Acts of the Apostles.

The two vertical pieces of the wooden screen, between the window panels, contain twelve crowns each, for a total of twenty-four. These indicate the twenty-four elders who surround the throne of God in the vision of John in the Book of Revelation. The chapter on the Revelation window elaborates on this symbol of the twenty-four crowns.

A vine, heavy with clusters of grapes, frames the window panels. The words of Jesus on the night of his arrest supply their meaning. Jesus compared himself to the vine, his Father to the vinedresser, and the disciples to the branches. Jesus encouragingly explains that his disciples will bear much fruit if Jesus abides in them and they abide in Jesus.

The final motif is that of the flowers and thistles which decorate the fretwork of the edging. Isaiah's prophecy that the desert will bloom as a rose at the Messiah's coming explains the flowers and the thistles point to the Presbyterian Church's roots in Scotland.

THE CHANCEL

The chancel is the elevated portion at the front of the church which includes seating for the choir and clergy, the retable or reredos, the Lord's table or communion table, lectern, pulpit, and baptismal font. Other elements in the chancel are the cross, the candles, and the paraments. Each of the furnishings in the chancel is a reminder of the elements of worship, referred to collectively as "Word and Sacrament."

The focal point for the worshiping congregation is the great symbol of Christianity, the cross. It is a reminder that Jesus Christ is the center of the Christian faith. The cross is shown empty as a reminder of Christ's resurrection.

Behind and above the Lord's table is the reredos. A silver cross, candlesticks, and flowers rest on the reredos shelf. Stylized roses are carved around the shelf and represent the Messianic promise of Christ.

The five-foot silver cross stands on the shelf of the towering retable or reredos, the elaborate carved wooden, gold and stained glass backdrop of scenic panels forming the rear of the chancel. The candles on the shelf are reminders that Jesus is the Light of the world and remind worshipers that they too are called to be light in the world. Occasionally flowers are also placed on the retable to commemorate an event in the life of the church or of a church member, such as a wedding or funeral, but nothing ever hides the cross.

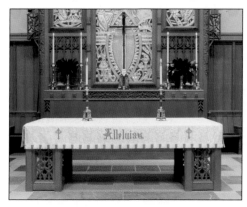

The Lord's table sits on the top step in the center of the chancel, covered with a white brocade frontal appliquéd with Alleluia in the center front and flanked with Celtic crosses. The two candles on the table represent Jesus' human and divine natures. White is the color usually used to celebrate communion, weddings and funerals.

Also in a central place in the chancel is the communion table, sometimes called the Lord's or people's table. In Protestant Reformed churches there is no altar. The Lord's table is a reminder of Jesus' invitation to participate in the fellowship of God. The elements of the Lord's supper, or communion, are prepared there. The offering plates may be placed there as a symbol of the worshipers' sacrificial response to God's redeeming love shown in Jesus Christ.

The font has an octagonal or eight-sided base representing regeneration and new life.

The Gothic style baptismal font stands in the center of the chancel. It is a reminder of God's adoption of believers into his family, a sign of his covenant with his people. The font holds water that the minister sprinkles on the head of the one being baptized.

The lectern stands to the right front of the chancel. The Bible rests here each Sunday after a family from the congregation carries it in during the processional.

Scripture is read and prayers are offered here. It reminds worshipers of God's revelation of himself in the Bible.

Carved on the front of the lectern is the Chi Rho symbol, an ancient sacred monogram of Christ used by early Christians as a secret sign of their faith.

The pulpit front features a carved pomegranate atop an empty Latin cross.

The pulpit stands to the left front of the chancel. It is here that Scripture is proclaimed and applied. On the front of the pulpit is a pomegranate carved on top of an empty Latin cross. Because of its multitude of seeds, the pomegranate is symbolic of the resurrection and of the many believers who are members of the church universal.

THE COLOR AND ART OF WORSHIP

The Lord's table, the pulpit and the lectern may be adorned with decorative cloths called paraments. The background color indicates the season of the church year and the symbols serve as a reminder of the theme of the season or event.

For over a thousand years, the church paid little attention to the use of color. Calvinists in the 16th century saw no value in color and abolished its use in church furnishings. Black was used until the 19th and 20th centuries when Protestants, recognizing the value of engaging the eyes as well as the ears of worshipers, began to use liturgical colors to correspond with the church liturgical year.

The church liturgical year celebrates the mighty acts of God based on the birth, life, death, and resurrection of Jesus Christ. The church year includes Advent, Christmas, Epiphany, Lent, Easter, and Pentecost.

Advent begins the new church year on the Sunday nearest November 30 (St. Andrew's Day) and continues for four Sundays ending on Christmas Eve. The traditional color of Advent, a time of joyful anticipation, is purple or blue.

Christmas season begins Christmas Day and continues for 12 days through January 5. This is a season of great joy in celebration of the birth of Jesus Christ, the incarnation of God. The color of Christmas is white or gold.

Epiphany season begins on January 6 and varies in length depending on the date set for Easter. With the exception of Easter, Epiphany has been celebrated as a church holy day longer than any other. Epiphany means "to be made manifest". It is an observance of the coming of the Magi or Wise Men of the East as the manifestation of Jesus to the whole world. The liturgical color of Epiphany is white or gold.

The season of Lent lasts forty-six days beginning on Ash Wednesday and ending on the eve of Easter. Lent is characterized as a time of personal reflection and repentance; for some it is a time of personal sacrifice or denial. The last week of Lent is Holy Week, which begins with Palm Sunday. Thursday of Holy Week is called Maundy Thursday and commemorates the Last Supper. Good Friday of Holy Week is an observance of Jesus' crucifixion. The liturgical color of Lent is purple. Black is substituted on Good Friday.

Easter season begins on Easter Sunday and continues for 50 days until Pentecost. It is the oldest of Christian festival days and the most joyful as it is a celebration of Christ's resurrection. Easter is set as the first Sunday after the first full moon on or following March 21. Because of this lunar timing Easter continues to correspond with the Jewish season of Passover, just as it did on the first Easter. The liturgical color for Easter is white.

Pentecost means "fiftieth day" and is the beginning of the longest season of the church year. It lasts until the first Sunday of Advent. On Pentecost the Holy Spirit descended upon the disciples in Jerusalem, empowering them to preach to people from every nation. The writer of Acts speaks of 3,000 being added to their number that day. Christians have considered this event to be the founding of the church. The liturgical color of Pentecost is red, the liturgical color for the Sundays following Pentecost is green.

101

Needlepoint stoles are worn by the pastors to correspond with the colors of the church seasons.

Covering the communion table is a white brocade frontal appliquéd with "In Remembrance of Me" and flanked by fleur-de-lis crosses symbolizing the Holy Trinity and the resurrection.

This handmade, cutwork and needlework white communion cloth was given to MPPC as a gift by its sister church, the Great Church of Debrecen, Hungary, in 2000.

These four stacked silver communion trays are covered with a top adorned by a version of a Maltese cross, whose eight points symbolize regeneration. The large engraved silver chalice, a memorial gift, is used each communion Sunday. The chalice is a symbol of communion and the forgiveness of sin won by the blood of Christ. The silver bread trays with handmade white linen liners are used in each communion service.

Two of the silver offering plates with handmade needlepoint silencers depict various flower and fruit designs. Some plates are plain and others are engraved, "it is more blessed to give than to receive."

The silver memorial containers above and below are used on the retable for flowers.

A large silver pitcher is used during communion to symbolize the "pouring out the blood of Jesus Christ" into the chalice. Another silver chalice with a shield on its side, perhaps depicts a stylized cross of the apostle Andrew. A silver bread tray has a white linen liner.

A handmade pottery chalice and bread plate are decorated with grapes and the Latin cross. The grapes symbolize communion, the blood shed by Jesus on the cross and also symbolize the fruitfulness of the Christian life. The empty Latin cross is a reminder of the resurrection and the hope of eternal life. This chalice and plate are part of a collection of ceramic and pottery chalices and plates often used when communion is served by intinction.

In the chancel are twelve moveable choir chairs with handmade needlepoint seats and backs. The seat features a harp in the center of a shield surrounded by olive branches on a blue background. The back shows horns crossed and entwined with ribbon on which is written "Gloria." The harp represents the Psalms and all music and instruments that are used to praise and glorify God. The olive branches symbolize peace. Blue often represents heaven, or truth.

This handmade needlepoint bench is used for weddings. The center symbol is a stylized sacred monogram for Christ, the Chi Rho, the first two letters of the Greek word for Christ. The fleur-de-lis crosses on either side serve as reminders of the Trinity and the resurrection. All three crosses are entwined with lily of the valley representing Christ's birth and new life. The holly leaves represent Christ's Passion.

On this large white brocade pall, the Chi Rho symbol is encircled by a gold shield in the center.

This large light blue handmade needlepoint pall is in the form of a cross with Christian symbols and flowers. Blue often represents heaven. The Holy Trinity is symbolized by the fleur-de-lis, and Jesus Christ by the Alpha and Omega. The dove signifies peace, while resurrection is symbolized by the lilies, pomegranates, and butterflies. The central symbol, a cross and crown, is symbolic of both Christ's victory over death, and the crown of life promised to all who love the Lord and are faithful until death (James 1:12, Revelation 2:10). It can be used alone to cover a casket or with a simple white covering underneath.

The large crucifer is centered with one of the sacred monograms of Jesus, IHS, consisting of the first three letters of the Greek word for Jesus. The crucifer is carried down the center aisle of the church on Sunday mornings. It precedes the choir and is placed near the retable or reredos. Following the service, it is carried down the center aisle of the church preceding the choir.

105

The winged lion represents St. Mark. A Jerusalem cross is on the left and a stylized Chi Rho is on the right.

A white linen cloth with a handmade embroidered shell design covers the baptismal table. The pitcher holding the water for baptism sits on the table. The shell, often a scallop or cockle shell, is a symbol of baptism, particularly the baptism of Christ. Shells are often shown with three drops of water to represent the Trinity.

Four benches in the Narthex have handmade needlepoint seats symbolizing the Four Evangelists as derived from Ezekiel's vision. The figures hold books representing the New Testament and have wings representing the spread of the Gospel to all the earth.

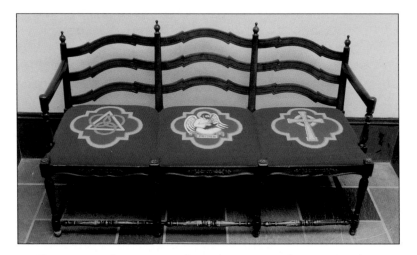

The winged man represents St. Matthew. To the left is a dual symbol of interlocked circles and a triangle both representing the Trinity of one God in three persons. To the right is a Celtic or Irish cross, one of the oldest cruciforms.

The winged ox represents St. Luke. To the left is a sacred monogram formed from the first three letters of the Greek word for Jesus. To the right is the five pointed star symbolizing Jesus' incarnation at Bethlehem.

The winged eagle represents St. John. To the left is a stylized budded cross representing the Trinity which is encircled by a crown signifying Christ, the King of

kings. To the right is the sacred monogram of Alpha and Omega, the first and last letters of the Greek alphabet, the symbol of eternity. Above it is another crown.

THE ORGANS

The Myers Park Presbyterian Church organ was built in 1961 by the Canadian firm, Casavant Frères, one of the world's premier pipe organ builders. The Casavant company, established in 1879, is the oldest continuing name in North America organ building. The organ in our sanctuary is actually two separate instruments each with its own console: the balcony organ, consisting of 15 stops, is played from a two manual and pedal console. The chancel organ, consisting of 47 stops, is played from a three manual and pedal console.

It is also possible to play the balcony organ from the chancel console. This is possible because of the electropneumatic action of the instrument. This is in contrast to direct mechanical connections, which require that the pipes be placed above the keyboards. The tonal scheme is reminiscent of 19th century French instruments.

GLOSSARY OF TERMS

Aureole – an elongated nimbus, or halo, surrounding an entire figure – generally restricted to Jesus or the Virgin Mary and the Christ child

Chancel – the elevated, enclosed portion at the front of our sanctuary

Cherubim – plural of cherub, a winged celestial being

Chi-Rho – the ancient monogram of Christ, consisting of the first two letters of Christ in the Greek language

Creator's Star – a six pointed star made up of two interlocking triangles which symbolizes the six days of creation.

Cruciform Nimbus – see tri-radiant nimbus

Façade – the front, particularly decorative, of a building

Fasces of the lictor – an ax bound with rods which was carried before the chief magistrate by a lictor (attendant) in ancient Rome – typical symbol of the Roman government

IHS (or IHC) – a sacred monogram, an abbreviation of the Greek word IHCOYC, meaning Jesus. The use of this as an anagram, "*Iesus hominum salvator*" Latin for "Jesus, Savior of mankind", is a more recent mid-15th century development.

Lancet – a high narrow window – each of the large stained glass windows in the Sanctuary is divided into two lancets

Lumiere – a black and white line drawing of a stained glass window's detail and design

Manus Dei – Latin for "The hand of God"

Nimbus – halo

Seraphim – angelic creatures with three pairs of wings, one pair with which they cover their face, another to fly, and a third to cover their feet

Star of David – a six-pointed star currently used as a modern-day symbol of Israel

Synoptic gospels – the first three gospels of the New Testament, so called because of their many similarities

Tracery – ornamental architectural work used at the top of Gothic windows

Tri-radiant nimbus – a halo with three rays within, strictly reserved for use with any one of the Trinity: Father, Son, or Holy Spirit

Vesica piscis aureole – an upright, oblong, pointed aureole which is used to surround figures and symbols of Christ

INDEX OF BIBLICAL CHARACTERS

109

INDEX OF SYMBOLS

110

SOURCES

Scripture quotations are from the *New Revised Standard Version* except as indicated on page 3.

Ferguson, George. Signs & Symbols in Christian Art.
    London: Oxford University Press, 1961.

Gast, Walter E. "Symbols in Christian Art And
    Architecture." Internet. June 2000
    ⟨http://home.att.net/~wegast/ symbols/
    symbols.htm⟩

Webber, F.R. Church Symbolism. Detroit:
    Omnigraphics, 1992.

With special gratitude we also acknowledge:

Henry Willet: Iconography Sanctuary Windows
        Myers Park Presbyterian Church

The Reverend James E. Fogartie: Iconography
        Monthly Session Meeting, April 1961

Eleanor Belk: Stained Glass Windows Guide
        Myers Park Presbyterian Church

ACKNOWLEDGEMENTS

Sanctuary Book Committee

Chairman
Lois Alexander

Editors
Sandy DuPuy
Katherine Forney
Lori Griswold
Kim Stump

Writers
Eleanor "Babbie" Boyd – Paraments, Communion
    Service & Linens
Beth Jackson – Paraments, Communion Service &
    Linens
Betty Mulliss – Paraments, Communion Service &
    Linens
Ann & Bob Stigall – Musical Instruments
Kim Stump – Stained Glass Windows

Cover & Layout
Coco Killian

Photographs
Gordon Schenck

Consultants
Margaret Bigger
Betsy Johnson
William R. Peterson
Elizabeth Tucker

Proof Readers
Brevard Alexander, Jr.
Sharon Houston
Lucielle Hunter
Kathy McCollum
Missy Plyler
Pam Stowe
Walt Summerville, Jr.

Church Staff
The Rev. Dr. Steven P. Eason
The Rev. Dr. Eldon Von Clemens
Fay Grasty, Presbyterian Women Advisor

Presbyterian Women
Dana Marshall, Moderator
Sarah Bailey, Treasurer

A special thank you to the families of committee members for their patience and encouragement while this book was written. Sincere and heartfelt thanks go to Helene Weiss, head librarian of Willet Stained Glass Studios, who provided invaluable insights into the design, creation, and symbolism of the windows. Other thanks go to Rita Pleimann and Sherry Clontz of Jostens for their considerable help.